Carina Contini and her husband Victor opened their first restaurant on George Street in Edinburgh in 2004, celebrating their Italian Scots heritage. They run three award-winning restaurants and recently received two prestigious listings from Accademia Italiana Della Cucina. Carina is passionate about food and maintains a high profile in the food and drinks industry. She has written for *The Scotsman* for more than 12 years and regularly contributes to *The Herald* and BBC Scotland.

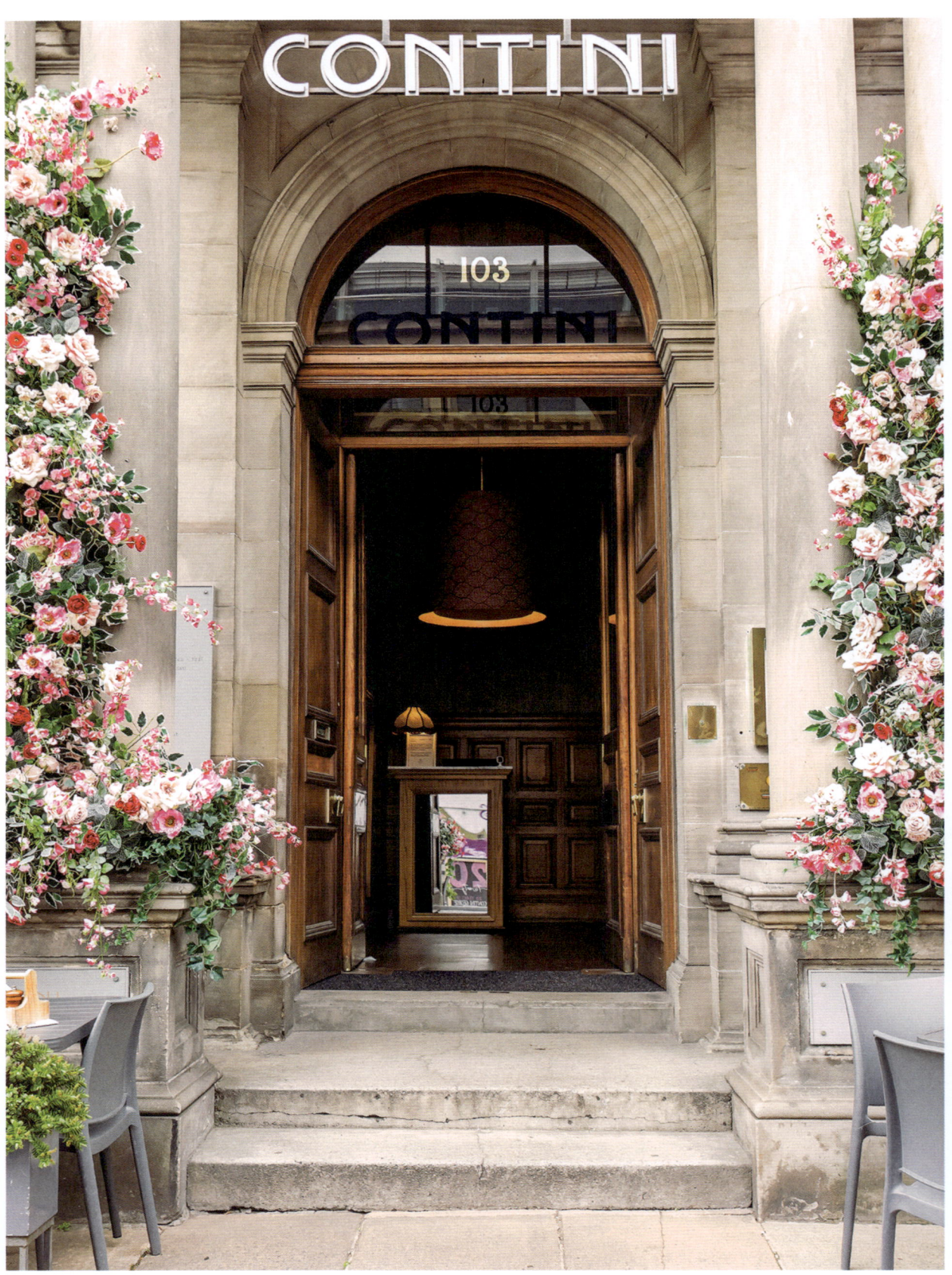

The CONTINI COOKBOOK

Carina Contini

BIRLINN

First published in 2024 by
Birlinn Limited
West Newington House
10 Newington Road
Edinburgh
EH9 1QS

www.birlinn.co.uk

Copyright © Carina Contini 2024

Food photography © Ambar Dandrea Photography
(www.ambardandreaphotography.com)

The right of Carina Contini to be identified as the author of this work has been asserted by her in accordance with the Copyright, Designs and Patents Act 1988.

All rights reserved. No part of this publication may be reproduced, stored or transmitted in any form without the express written permission of the publisher.

ISBN: 978 1 78027 921 3

British Library Cataloguing-in-Publication Data
A catalogue record for this book is available from the British Library

Design by Mark Blackadder

Papers used by Birlinn are from well-managed forests and other responsible sources

Printed and bound by Bell & Bain Ltd, Glasgow

*Dedicated to
Nonna G, my mother,
who taught me not to stir the sugo
when someone else was cooking.
With much love, No. 8*

CONTENTS

Welcome 9

A day in the life of our restaurants 15

Integrity 21

Larder notes 25

Piccoli Piatti

Frittelle 33
Fritti 35
Carpaccio di Pesce 37
Mozzarella in Carrozza 38
Polenta con Fontina 40
Polpette 41
Pastone 42
Bruschetta 45
Aperitivi 50
    Mandorle Speziate 50
    Noci con Miele 50
    Contini Olives 50
Arancini 53

Zuppe

Minestra 57
Pasta e Fagioli 58
Minestrone 59
Zuppe di Pesce 60
Crema di Pomodoro 63
Crema di Funghi 64
Zuppe di Lenticchie 65
Brodo 67
Brodo di Carne 68
Ceci e Patate 73

Pasta

Homemade Pasta 76
Pasta al Pomodoro 79
Pasta ai Peperoni 81
Broccoletti 83
Spaghetti con Tonno 84
Gnocchi Cacio e Pepe 88
Carbonara 91
Contadino 92
Amatriciana 94
Puttanesca 95
Linguine ai Frutti di Mare 96

Pesce

Scampi 101
Capesante 102
Calamari Fritti 103
Merluzzo 105
Branzino 106
Sgombro 109
Cozze 113
Pesce al Forno 114
Granchio 115
Pesce al Taglio 116
Aragosta 119

Carne

Ragù 125
Ossobuco 126
Fegato alla Veneziana 129
Coniglio all'Ischitana 131
Milanese 132
Salsiccia 135
Bollito Misto 136
Pollo 139
Porchetta 140
Stufato di Capra al Pecorino 143

Contorni

Crema di Cannellini	149
Zucca	150
Verdure	151
Melanzane alla Parmigiana	152
Asparagi	155
Frittata Verde	156
Spinaci	158
Carciofi	159
Galletti	161
Peperoni	162

Insalate

Crudi	166
Radicchio di Treviso	167
Anguria e Caprino	169
Arancia	172
Zucchini	175
Melograno	176
Fave	179
Puntarelle	180
Cavolfiore	181
Mozzarella di Bufala	182
Panzanella	185

Dolci

Macedonia	188
Torta di Fichi e Mandorle	189
Torta di Pistacchio	191
Cassata	192
Tiramisù	195
Panna Cotta	196
Panettone Pudding	199
Strudel	202
Zabaglione	204
Torta al Cioccolato	205

Pane, Torte & Biscotti

Focaccia	209
Pizza al Taglio	210
Pandolce	213
Bombolone	214
Bignè al Cioccolato e Ciliegie	217
Biscotti al Pecorino	219
Mandorle	220
Finocchio	223
Torta di Ricotta	224
Baci	229

Bevande

Fragola Fra	232
Notte Nocino	233
Negroni	235
Anguria	236
Pompelmo	236
Spritz	239
Vin Brulé	240
Espresso Martini	240
Vini	243
Digestivi	248

Posso lasciare la tavola?	251
Index	252

Dear lovely people,

All my life I've had one dilemma: am I Italian or Scottish?

To a Scot, my name suggests I'm Italian. To an Italian, my name suggests something else. As the youngest of eight children, my parents struggled to name me. The story goes that my paternal grandmother said, 'Call her Carina,' which translates to 'little darling'. Living up to the name is a whole other story.

Victor, my darling husband, also a second generation Italian Scot, feels the same. His Italian is far better than mine, but he always feels it's not quite good enough.

What I'm describing is the immigrant challenge: when you're not the first generation trying to find its way, but the second or third generation trying to feel at home.

For my family, 2019 was a significant year. It marked 100 years from when my paternal grandfather, Nonno Cesidio, arrived in Scotland to make a new home for his family. My father, a babe in arms, and his elder sister, Carmella, arrived a few months later in early 1920 with his mother.

I always thought that with a 100-year anniversary under our belts we would finally feel Scottish, but it's not happened yet. To the stranger in the street, we are Scottish. Our accents are. We are welcomed as natives – something we treasure and value dearly – but we still feel like outsiders, looking in. Brexit Britain has made this more emotive.

Surprisingly, our children feel the same. Like us, they were born in Edinburgh. They feel Scots Italian, while my generation describe themselves as Italian Scots. Maybe it's merging slowly.

Our heritage has left such a strong mark on who we are. It threads all the way through to the clothes we wear, the music we listen to, the cars we want to drive (currently a Fiat but Victor's still holding out for the Ferrari) and, most importantly, how we eat.

When asked if I'm Italian or Scottish, I say I cook Italian, but I love and am happy and content to live in Scotland. Scotland is home for the body and soul; maybe Italy is home for the heart and the stomach.

The food that feeds my children and is abundant on our table is instinctively Italian. Being an Italian cook for me is about choosing the best, freshest ingredients, knowing where everything comes from, and using all my energy to share a delicious meal with the people we love and, of course, with our wonderful customers.

The same philosophies and values that run through our family life run through our business life. We don't know where one stops and the other starts.

When Nonno Cesidio arrived in Scotland, he learned to make ice cream and fry fish and chips for the beautiful people of Cockenzie. A century later we're doing the same – sourcing the best ingredients, preparing them as freshly as we can and sharing them with the beautiful locals and visitors of Edinburgh: fish and chips and 100 per cent Scottish ingredients at The Scottish Cafe & Restaurant, and Italian ingredients and delights at Contini George Street. Cannonball Restaurant's strong Scottish heritage has a little of the Auld Alliance enhancing its cooking styles.

This book shares my bible of recipes, connecting my family and Victor's. They make me feel Italian even when I'm in Scotland, and prove my Italian origins whenever I get to cook. They're enriched with more than 30 years of travelling and learning the identities of Italy's amazing regions. Some of our favourite places in Italy, with some holiday snaps, are shared throughout the book, alongside recipes that spark a memory of food eaten and enjoyed. You'll find Italian-style strudel from up in the Alps, all the way down to a fragrant bowl of cozze from Campania.

The healthy Mediterranean diet is at the heart of how we eat. Preserved and cured foods provide the backbone of a culture of seasonal harvests: making things last until you need their nutrients. Tradition, often indoctrinated by religion, also influences our cooking, with Christmas and Easter as anchors to keep us eating together en masse. We might have stopped going to church, but we've not lost the excuse for a party.

Biodiversity meets sustainability when you describe the topography and the agricultural and farming traditions of countries like Scotland and Italy. Nurture nature and nature will nurture us. Everything needs to be considered. If you respect the season, our food heritage gets to shine and our diet benefits hugely with a vast array of different flavours that make eating exciting. Ultra-processed food, not meat, in our world is the issue. It's never been a part of our habits. Sugar consumption is a problem; it's my own addiction. My sweet tooth has a will of its own. I just love to bake and I constantly battle to moderate my intake of sugary sins.

Living in Scotland means eating well is easy in spring, summer and autumn. Over the winter it's a challenge. You have to learn to be creative and maybe make some not so sustainable choices as a balance to maintaining sanity on your plate.

Part of what makes our restaurant at Contini George Street so Italian is our produce. We import fresh vegetables and fruit direct from the market in Milan each week. The produce is delivered by road and we believe it's the sustainable choice to bring sunshine to Scotland, particularly in the winter months. The lorries head back to Europe usually filled with the best of Scotland's own larder.

We recently received two awards from the Accademia Italiana della Cucina, the Italian Academy of Cuisine: a TTT grade award and, from the Academy board, il Diploma di Buona Cucina, a certificate that is awarded to those restaurants, in Italy as well as abroad, which work to maintain the Italian tradition and high quality in their cuisine.

'Love happy food' has always been our motto. Good food enjoyed together with family and friends. I'm delighted to share the recipes that my family love, and I love to cook for them. I hope they become part of your family's favourites, too.

In 2004, when Victor and I opened our first restaurant without any wider family involvement, the address was 103 George Street. Many of you will know our restaurant as Centotre. We changed the name as so many struggled to say it correctly (sometimes I wish we hadn't, but hey ho). We celebrate the good luck this number has brought us over the last 20 years, with over 103 recipes to match the years of cooking and sharing what Italian food means to me.

Keep well, and happy cooking.

CONTINI
GEORGE STREET, EDINBURGH

BREAKFAST

Breakfast Negroni £10
Freshly squeezed orange juice with Campari and Martini Rosso

FRESH JUICES AND MORNING COCKTAILS

FRESHLY PRESSED ORANGE JUICE SML £3.75 / LRG £5

FRESHLY PRESSED PINK GRAPEFRUIT JUICE
SML £3.75 / LRG £5

LAPRIG VALLEY APPLE JUICE £4.50

VIRGIN MOJITO £7
Laprig Valley Apple Juice muddled with fresh mint
and lime, crushed ice and topped up with soda

APEROL SPRITZ £11
Aperol, soda and prosecco, served with a slice of orange

GARIBALDI £10
Carina's all time favourite. Campari shaken with
freshly squeezed orange juice, served over ice

BLOODY MARY £10
Below vodka, tomato juice, freshly squeezed Amalfi
lemon juice, Tabasco, worcester sauce and black pepper

PROSECCO MIMOSA ROSMARINO £10
Victor & Carina Contini Prosecco with
freshly squeezed orange juice

LIGHTER BREAKFAST

BREAKFAST SALAD (NGCI GF OPTIONAL) £7
Italian fruit selection with Graham's Dairy Skyr
yoghurt, Victor's honey and granola

ORGANIC PORRIDGE (NGCI GF OPTIONAL) £8
Double cream or coconut milk organic porridge

WITH YOUR CHOICE OF
Stewed Italian plum and roasted almond flakes
OR
Poached Italian pear and toasted hazelnuts

COOKED BREAKFAST

TOASTED SOURDOUGH WITH GRIERSON'S ORGANIC POACHED
OR SCRAMBLED EGGS

Stornoway black pudding and wilted spinach leaves
£10.50
Kaizen smoked sea trout and fresh dill
(NGCI OPTIONAL) £14
Ramsay of Carluke bacon and grilled Italian tomato
(NGCI OPTIONAL) £10
Grilled courgette, sun dried tomatoes and Parmigiano
Reggiano DOP (NGCI OPTIONAL) £10

SCOTTISH FULL-COOKED BREAKFAST £16
Full Scottish breakfast with Crombies pork sausage,
Ramsay of Carluke bacon, Grierson's organic poached eggs,
Stornoway black pudding, mushrooms and grilled
San Marzano tomato.
Served with chargrilled sourdough and butter

ADD A GLASS OF FRESHLY PRESSED ORANGE JUICE £3.75

VEGETARIAN FULL-COOKED BREAKFAST £14
Grierson's organic poached eggs, spinach, Italian
courgettes, peppers, mushrooms and grilled tomato. Served
with chargrilled sourdough and butter

ADD A GLASS OF FRESHLY PRESSED ORANGE JUICE £3.75

PLANT BASED BREAKFAST (PB) (NGCI OPTIONAL) £12
Chilli roasted Italian violet aubergine, courgettes,
peppers and sweet onions with Taggiasche olives
and fresh Kitchen Garden lovage crumb. Served with
chargrilled sourdough drizzled with EVOO

DOLCE BRUNCH £14

Au Gourmand buttery with Ramsay of Carluke bacon,
seasonal berries, maple syrup and Katy Rodgers creme
fraiche

BUTTER...
Our beautiful Aberdeen...
by Au Gourmand Bakery...

TROUT...
Kaizen smoked sea trout...
eggs, hollandaise sauce...

SPECK DI PROS...
Speck di Prosciutto D...
poached eggs and hol...

FLORENTIN...
Pan fried spinach, Grier...
hollandaise sauce...

WORLD FAMOUS...

Double cream sco...
Grilled San...
Pan frie...
Crombies...
Stornoway...
Ramsay of...

1 FILLING £7 - 2 FILL...

PASTI...

Homemade fruit scone, str...
Homemade cheese scone...
Homemade so...
Au Gourmand Aberdeen butt...
and homemade Italian...

A DAY IN THE LIFE OF OUR RESTAURANTS

At Contini George Street, we say we are a hotel without rooms.

The doors open to the public at 9 a.m. but the kitchen team arrives around 6 a.m. Majeck, our head pastry chef, joined in 2006, two years after we opened. Good kitchens have consistency. Having a team that's been with us for years is a huge blessing. Focaccia, bomboloni, jam, marmalade, gelato, sorbetto, cakes and fresh pasta are made every day. The seasonality of our menus will show through in these dishes.

We've always been a venue for breakfast – something I love – whether it's the suits making the deals, or the tech team with their Friday coffee morning. Mike Coulter, of the original Edinburgh Coffee Morning Brigade, and his entourage hold a special place in our hearts. We're here for everyone.

The front of house team arrives an hour before we open to set the restaurant. The coffee machine stays on all day and all night, so we can have caffeine anytime. Cocktails are a fashion and a passion of the team. Drinks are served on the tables opposite the bar. We call this the Italian Bar. In the best Italian style, you're more than welcome to prop up the bar like Victor, enjoying his morning coffee, chatting to 'Marcus Aurelius', lovely Marc, our bar manager.

Victor is our Mr Culture and the basis of our Victor Welcome training. He's the heart of our business. The team and the customers love him. I love him – after 30 years of marriage, it would be hard not to.

He's also our Mr Italy. His phone is the control centre for all our Italian orders, Brexit bamboozlement, logistics, customs and, most vitally, the relationships that enable us to buy direct from Italy. This has been a truly unique part of what we've done since day one. Victor works in real time through WhatsApp, usually around midnight when we're in bed. It's never dull seeing the first kaki or borlotti beans of the season. It's a huge task, and as my Italian isn't half good enough I couldn't do it. It's all done in Italian. We can't get this produce any fresher. The orecchiette for our Contadino pasta is made in Puglia and sent to Milan to be added to the transport. Mozzarella di bufala from a *caseificio* in Campania, burrata from Puglia and Parmigiano Reggiano from Emilia-Romagna all arrive separately to the dispatch point to be added to our pallet.

Opposite: Bombolone (p. 214)

Victor loves all the new season extravaganzas, like white Alba truffles from Piemonte, the first pressing of olive oil from my brother in Italy, panettone and pandoro at Christmas from Cuneo. He's our Man from Del Mercato. I should buy him a hat.

Small fragile items, like truffles, will be dispatched by air freight. But for the big orders, it's all by road. Our little restaurant is involved in grand logistics.

Menus are printed for each service after the teams have a catch-up. Alina, our favourite, who's been with us for double digit years, runs the restaurants, the teams and chooses the wines with a guiding palate from Victor. When we draft a menu or list, we think of our friends, family and customers. Remembering what they like and love is an essential part of bringing balance to what we serve. It's very personal.

Lunch service over, all the team get their break. They eat together and get to chill before aperitivo time arrives for our customers, that wonderful Milanese institution of sipping a Negroni or Spritz with some classic nibbles. Dinner service starts from 5 p.m.

The financial stuff – I'm calling it 'stuff' because it's not the love of running a restaurant but is a necessity – is done by Caroline and Emma. They have supported and looked after us for years, allowing us to focus on the really important stuff, like the customers, the product and the team. How do our guests feel? Did they receive the Victor Welcome? Was our Magnificent Seven front of house and back of house delivered to ensure a good meal is an excellent experience? Did we give the Carlo Cuddle? The thank you. Have we shared our values clearly enough? These are all parts of our development that have grown organically and are now held through our Contini Training Academy. Thanks to Emma, our HR manager, for holding this.

103 George Street is a former banking hall designed from a Florentine palazzo. Built in 1876, its classical architecture, with Corinthian columns, ornate gilded plasterwork and 18-foot ceilings, makes it feel Italian.

Italian lessons have always played in our washrooms and there is always someone on the floor to share a little Italiano practice.

I've never had an office. Even at home, my office is the kitchen table. At work it's one of the restaurant tables. I apologise in advance, I always say; you'll find me where there is a problem. If you don't see me, that's a good thing. The team does far better without me interfering (stirring the sugo).

We can't do anything without our team. I can say with all humility that we are better employers now than when we started. There is no price for experience. We've learned how to nurture and engage with our team as the business has become more established. The old saying 'if I knew then what I know now' comes to mind, but the better one is 'it's only by learning that we live a full life'. I sometimes regret that we didn't have a full-time mentor. The upside is we got here under our own steam, which has its own rewards. We're better with the team we have around us. We couldn't do what we do without them: Attila, Agha, Stephanie – too many to mention everyone.

Seasonality brings more excitement. We look forward to April, when we start dressing the terraces. We're very fortunate we have such amazing street spaces. Whether you're sitting looking at Edinburgh Castle, breathing in East Princes Street Gardens or just watching the *passeggiata* and buzz of George Street, you get the feel of the heart and soul of our beautiful city. The summer comes and brings the Festival. December brings our Christmas decorations. Edinburgh, we love you.

The seasons also bring our flavours. At George Street, these celebrate the sunshine of Italy and make us feel like we're on holiday when we've come to work. Figs, puntarelle, peaches, apricots, Abate pears, cherries, scarola, chestnuts, artichokes, Amalfi lemons, Tarocco oranges . . . the list is endless. I can tell the month of the year by looking at old menus just based on the ingredients. Fresh, simple Italian at its best. Scottish ingredients are equally important: asparagus, strawberries, wild garlic and chanterelles, not to mention all the fresh fish, shellfish, and great meat and game.

When the last guests leave and all the cleaning is complete, the EOD – 'end of day' – report shares the service story. It's a record of sales, weather, team and customer comments. It's a great tool to make better decisions. Only when this comes in do I switch my phone off. It's a strange life, hospitality. We want you to feel relaxed, but a whole load of energy goes on in the background. This keeps us fit and healthy, and we hope to be able to cook and share good food and look after you for many, many years to come.

Thank you most sincerely. Without you in our lives, we wouldn't be able to do what we all love.

Carina & Victor

INTEGRITY

It seems strange to start a family cookbook with a chapter on food fraud, so I renamed this *integrity*.

When you buy food (or get the bill in a restaurant), quality and authenticity of the product (as much as the full service experience) should be reflected in the price. Without understanding the journey of food, it's often difficult to understand the real value or its integrity. Food fraud and clever marketing confuse us.

The classification of food and wine around the world is a vitally important part of protecting the integrity of heritage foods. Provenance is a key ingredient. It protects the end product, the land where it's produced and, importantly, the people who produce it. Good food should be simple, but in a global world it is actually very complicated. Sadly, there is room for exploitation and the market is bombarded by fakes. Just like you can pick up a fake Gucci or Prada on the beach abroad, marketing has led to many fake foods appearing blatantly on our shelves, pretending to be the real McCoy. This confuses the consumer. Interestingly, Italy has started its own campaign against fake food – Fermiamo Il Falso Cibo Italiano (#NOFAKEINITALY) – as the problem is as big at source as it is abroad.

Olive oil, Prosciutto di Parma, Parmigiano Reggiano, Aceto Balsamico di Modena and some famous wines are just a few of the highest value Italian exports that have been exposed the most in terms of fraud or misleading branding.

To be clear, there is fraud and there is misleading branding. In law, they are different; in my world, they are the same and cause equal damage. Check the labels to make sure you are buying what you think you are paying for.

We are hugely passionate about olive oil because it is the foundation of our cooking. It also reminds me how lucky we are, having (and affording) one of the world's most special ingredients.

When I say extra virgin olive oil, it's always the first pressing single estate variety. Sometimes it's Tuscan or Puglian, or from Liguria, but mostly it's from my brother's farm in the Lazio mountains.

Olive oil can be anything from this single source first pressing, or multinational oils bottled in one location, or a second or third extract of another olive oil, or an extract of the olive oil production with added oils from other plants. Looks deceive. Nutritionally, environmentally, economically and culinarily they are different.

True olive oils as a health ingredient are unbeatable. The best oils will have a high polyphenol count and low acidity. Legally this must be below 2 per cent, but some of the champions have acidity levels of 0.2 per cent.

Opposite: Minestrone (p. 59)

Labels may showcase the tricolore flag, seemingly selling a premium Italian product. On closer inspection, the label is saying the product is bottled in Italy, not actually grown there. You don't need to be Inspector Montalbano to find text claiming 'product of many European nations'. This may still be an extra virgin olive oil, but its provenance isn't authentic.

Brexit has resulted in huge administration, which has added to cost. Premium products such as Parmigiano Reggiano are more expensive than they have ever been. You may start seeing Grana Padano, which is a younger and slightly different style of hard Italian cheese. It's still a quality product, but it's not the same product. Grana need only be aged for nine months, while Parmigiano must be aged for 12. We only buy Parmigiano Reggiano that has been aged for 18 months minimum.

Migrant labour in Italy is also a black cloud that affects the true value of food. Sadly, you don't need to dig deep to find exploitation.

'Let the buyer beware' has never been more relevant. Good food – what I call real food – costs. It's not always an easy choice to spend more money, but it's important to know what you are spending your money on.

Integrity can be expensive, but it will never give you a guilty conscience or indigestion.

Classifications of Food

Here are some Italian food terms that you may have seen.

DOP: Denominazione d'Origine Protetta (Protected Designation of Origin). This guarantees that the food is produced, processed and packed in a specific geographical zone, according to tradition that is regulated, such as Parmigiano Reggiano.

IGP: Indicazione Geografica Protetta (Protected Geographical Indication). This shows the quality or reputation of the food or condiment is linked to the place or region where it is produced, processed or prepared. Mortadella Bologna IGP would be one of my favourite IGPs.

STG: Specialità Tradizionale Garantite (Guaranteed Traditional Speciality). This refers to how something is made rather than where it is made or what it is made from. Only two products fall into this classification: pizza Napoletana and mozzarella.

LARDER NOTES

Butter

All butters are not equal. Different types of milk, production methods and even the time of year can create very different tastes in an ingredient as simple as churned milk to make butter. Graham's is one of Scotland's best readily available brands. I always buy the unsalted variety, which leaves you to add as much salt as you wish. Italian butters can be very cheesy, and I don't use them, even for cooking.

Eggs

Happy eggs are important for happy cooking, especially for happy baking. We only use organic eggs in the restaurants, either from Grierson or from Phantassie Farm. All our recipes use large eggs.

Fish

Fishmongers' shops, like butchers' shops, are special places. I always leave Welch's in Newhaven with at least two meals more than I had planned. A Saturday steamed or roasted fish, like sea bass or bream, for a sunshine meal, even when it's rainy. A huge bag of mussels for a fish soup the next day . . . then a few smoked haddock packed into my fridge for fishcakes for a Monday night supper. My Italian Scottish roots sit very well in a fishmonger's.

Flour

Choosing the correct flour is the first step. Plain, white and all-purpose are the same. Self-raising flour has an added raising agent and is used for baking. Pasta flour and bread or pizza flours have a higher gluten content needed to give elasticity to the dough. They may both be labelled '00', but the bread or pizza flour will have a slightly higher gluten content. Next you must check that the flour is within its date. Don't get caught out with old flour; it is as good as bad flour. Don't use it.

Meat

Buying fresh meat from a butcher is often more expensive than buying from a supermarket, but the quality is usually better. We're very lucky in Edinburgh to have several very good local butchers. Saunderson's is my favourite – I rely on them to get the kind of great cuts which are not available in any chill cabinet, along with expert advice and a friendly smile.

Olive Oil

This is our most precious ingredient. We use Sofia's Olive Oil, the oil made by my brother in I Ciacca, at home and in our kitchens for all our sugo, focaccia, pan work and dressings. It's a great all-rounder. We use other single estate oils from Tuscany when we're looking for a little more power. Capezzana, Selvapiana and Fontodi are three of our favourites. Harvests vary year to year, and olive oil prices can fluctuate hugely depending on the weather. For deep frying, I will use a processed olive oil, as the flavour is lighter and less overpowering. Price usually matches quality in both flavour and health benefits. Think of olive oil as an investment in your health. You're worth it!

Pepper

Our dear friends Para and his family in Kerala hand-harvest organic berries and sun-dry them to produce the most fragrant and aromatic black peppercorns (white peppercorns just have the skins removed). Having a good peppermill, with the correct milling setting, is as important as the ingredient.

Salt

We use two types of salt: fine table salt and a more natural sea salt, such as Maldon Sea Salt Flakes or Blackthorn Sea Salt. For everything except salting water for boiling pasta, or for dressing the rim of a frozen Margarita glass (recipe not included), I use Maldon. I'm not frightened to use as much as is required. I often describe myself as the salt in the business. Too little and something is missing, too much and who wants that – getting it just right takes practice. I'm learning to master this.

Tomatoes

Tinned tomatoes are a gift. If you have a family in Italy who preserve and jar their own tomatoes during the summer season and share them with you, I'm jealous. If you're like the majority of us and have to rely on a supermarket, look no further along the shelf than the brand Mutti. They really are consistently the best. Like everything else, you pay for quality, but these are worth it. The passata, in particular, is excellent. Victor's Aunty Gloria would only use these tomatoes. As for most things, she was right.

Opposite: Calamari Fritti (p. 103)

CIOCIARIA

When we travel to Italy, we're usually tourists. Our heritage (but maybe not our accents) makes our hearts feel like natives. The place our souls feel most at home is the region that will forever be the foundation for our family, our love of Italy and probably, most importantly, our fascination with good food.

Our family home, I Ciacca, is in Ciociaria, a mountainous area between Rome and Naples. Ciociaria comes from the Italian word *ciocie*, the leather-strapped and curled-toe slippers that were commonly worn by its people.

The area was established as Italy's first national park, Parco Nationale d'Abruzzo, Lazio e Molise, in 1921. Though I was born and brought up beside the sea in Scotland, my roots are very much on a beautiful mountain in Italy that's 2,500 feet above sea level.

When I think of the landscape of my home, I see picture perfect nature. It's so remote that the sky dominates and treetops cover everything else.

The colours of baby blue and grass green live in idyllic harmony. The trickle of a stream or small waterfall is never far away, but the sound of silence brings peace. It is an absolute contrast to most of the other places in Italy that we love to visit.

Walking and regenerating are what happen when you visit this home. Nature takes over and brings us back to life. It's a special place. It's also a reminder of how life can be simpler, less commercial, less needy.

This area, like many similar parts of Italy, has felt the effects of migration. The first round took place from the mid to the end of the nineteenth century. America, for many, was the final destination. We didn't make it past the tiny fishing village of Cockenzie on the east coast of Scotland.

Picinisco, the nearest town to I Ciacca, is built on a natural rock formation and from the piazza it's as if you're sitting above the clouds. It

is a little part of heaven, regardless of the season.

The vast majority of families who left Italy to come to Scotland, particularly Edinburgh, are descendants from Picinisco or its neighbouring villages. A diaspora of 200,000 Italian Scots are believed to be descendants of this area alone. You can arrive at any time of the day or night and there will always be someone who knows your family. At peak season you'll probably hear English (with a Scottish accent) before you'll hear Italian. You are never more than two minutes' walk from the countryside that almost cuddles you. The Highlands of Scotland are a sister or brother of these lands, there is no doubt about it. In summer it's hot, and in winter snow will cover every cliff edge and mountain top. It's beautiful.

When I was in my twenties, I went to Rome to study Italian before I started full-time work. Realising early on that I'm rubbish at languages, and feeling miserable, I headed up to Picinisco to visit my cousin, Pauline. I stayed in my grandmother's house on my own. The house hadn't been renovated since the 1950s and even trying to turn the shower on caused a short circuit of the kettle. The fig tree in the back garden provided breakfast and Pauline fed me everything else. We ate on their terrace, overlooking I Ciacca and the valley below, with hundreds of shooting stars overhead. The rest of the time I sat and read cookbooks. I didn't learn Italian, but I sure learned a lot about cooking Italian.

This region for me is not about my favourite restaurants, churches or museums; it's about my family, and the dishes I've inherited and learned to cook. We start every party with frittelle, deep-fried dough balls, and then finish with crustella, lightly fried pastry ribbons drizzled in honey or dusted with sugar. Both of these classic dishes are staples of this region. Every family will have their own variation. For me, they tell us where we started and where we always want to end. It's a special part of the world and we're lucky to call it our real home.

Piccoli Piatti

FRITTELLE

Enough, as an appetiser, for 5–6 people

650g strong white 00 bread or pasta flour

15g table salt

lots of freshly milled black pepper

12g fresh (or 6g dried) yeast

650ml warm water

1 tsp sugar

Frittelle are the Ferrari of the dough ball world, but they are as cheap to make as an old, rusty Fiat. A very southern delight, they are unquestionably my favourite taste of being an Italian Scot. My family's variation are made with baccalà (salt cod) and are called crespelle (see overleaf).

In the south of Italy, these are served in the best *trattorie* and *pizzerie* – you'll never get them in a *ristorante*.

To make the dough, place the flour in a large mixing bowl, add the salt and lots of freshly milled black pepper. Leave in a warm place. I place mine in my simmering oven until the flour is warm to the touch. Watch the bowl doesn't get too hot, as this will kill the yeast.

Mix the yeast, water and sugar together in a jug, ensuring there is at least an inch of room to allow the mixture to grow. Cover with cling film and leave to activate for about 15 minutes in a warm, draught-free place. Remove the cling film from the yeast mixture and stir. It should bubble.

Add the liquid to the warm flour and beat until you have a silky consistency. I've broken my KitchenAid doing this, so get a thick wooden spoon and a very strong arm and start beating the dough. I've broken a wooden spoon too, so be warned. It will take about 5 minutes until the dough is elastic. No. 1 son is my best sous chef for this task.

Cover with cling film and again leave in a warm, draught-free spot for about 45 minutes. I wrap the bowl in layers of tea towels, almost like a little baby in a crib. This allows the yeast to stay cosy and the batter to rise. Remove the cling film and beat the batter again for 1 or 2 minutes. If it looks too stiff, add a few tablespoons of warm water. Aim for the consistency of a thick, elastic, wet dough. You are ready to start frying.

To deep fry, you'll need 1 litre of light olive oil and a 20cm casserole pot. Gather a slotted spoon, a flat baking tray lined with a sheet of greaseproof paper and a jug of cold olive oil (to dip the spoon into).

Heat the oil until it reaches 188°C/370°F. Test it with a walnut-sized ball of the batter, which should bubble immediately when it touches the oil, but not spit. I scoop the mixture up with a dessertspoon dipped in cold oil.

Keep adding the balls of batter until the frying oil is covered but not overfilled. Balancing the temperature of the oil takes a little practice. You're aiming for a rolling stream of bubbles. The trick is to keep the oil at a constant temperature, so you need to add enough frittelle to help the others cook and not burn.

Each ball will take about 2–3 minutes to cook. Check they are crisp and golden. The centre should be fluffy and spongy, not wet. Remove from the oil and place on the greaseproof paper, then season with salt. Once cooled slightly, transfer to a pretty plate to serve. We eat them standing up in the kitchen – they rarely make it to the table.

Baccalà (Salt cod)

The dough can be stuffed with anchovies or fresh, blanched seaweed, a moreish and very common addition around Naples. We love them stuffed with baccalà. I make them for every family gathering: birthdays, Easter, Christmas . . . Any excuse, actually.

Salting cod is a very old Mediterranean tradition for preserving fish. It's believed to originate in Portugal, but it is a huge part of Italian cooking, from Venice to Naples.

The salted, dried fish needs to be soaked in several changes of water over a 24-hour to 48-hour period. The fish is then rinsed in more cold water and then simmered gently for about 15 minutes until tender. The length of soaking and cooking very much depends on the quality and age of fish you start with. Once the cod is cooked, allow to cool and then remove from the water. Clean the flesh by removing any skin and bones. Be extra attentive, as the bones are large, fine and lethal. Dress the flakes of cod with a little extra virgin olive oil, freshly chopped parsley, a little dried chilli, a few slices of fresh garlic and freshly milled black pepper. This on its own, as part of an antipasto, is a delicacy.

You need just a little of the filling – no more than the size of a grape. I usually just use my fingers, but be prepared – it's sticky and messy! If your sink is close by, even better, as you'll need to wash your hands regularly. Make sure the filling is wrapped in the dough, otherwise the edges will burn in the oil, as the filling is naturally more delicate than the batter.

Tip from the kitchen

Don't get distracted when you're frying. Be organised. Have all your utensils laid out before you start. The oil can catch very easily and if it sparks or spits it will burn. Keep your eyes on the prize and fry.

FRITTI
con Salsa di peperoncini

Serves 4–6 as a starter or side dish

Choose a selection of the following:

small cauliflower, broken into small pieces (but try not to crumble the florets)

violet aubergine, thinly sliced

fennel, cut into thin wedges

courgette, cut into pencils, and the flowers, if you are lucky enough to grow them

sweet Tropea white onion, cut into rings

For the batter

150g self-raising flour

75g cornflour

1 tsp baking powder

225ml chilled sparkling mineral water

For the Salsa di peperoncini

50g flat-leaf parsley, leaves only

50g fresh mint, leaves only

50g basil, leaves only

25g small capers in salt, rinsed to remove the salt

enough extra virgin olive oil to loosen the sauce

2–3 large fresh red chillies, seeds removed and very finely chopped

zest and juice of 1 unwaxed lemon

sea salt flakes, to taste

Deep-fried food feels like a guilt trip. Shallow-fried food feels like a treat. The Italians are great at doing both. Without them, we probably wouldn't have such a love for fish and chips.

Interestingly, I think when you deep fry food it absorbs less oil, so it's up to you how low you wish to go. I tend to end up in the deep end most of the time and have no regrets.

This is no healthy end of the frying spectrum, but a little as part of a sharing antipasto of mozzarella di bufala with tomatoes and basil, burrata with roasted grapes and hazelnuts, and slices of prosciutto crudo adds the finishing warm touch every time.

To deep fry, you'll need 1 litre of light olive oil and a 20cm casserole pot.

Blanch the cauliflower in boiling salted water until cooked. I like a slight bite to it. Drain and dry with a kitchen towel and set aside. The other vegetables can all be fried from raw.

In a large bowl, beat together the ingredients for the batter. Fill a casserole pot with the oil and heat until it reaches 188°C/370°F. Coat each piece of your chosen vegetable in the batter. This is messy, as the batter is quite wet. You can use tongs if you're a little timid frying. Gently dip the vegetable pieces into the oil. They should sizzle but not spit. Fry until golden, turning to make sure all sides are gently browned. Remove from the oil and allow to cool on a baking sheet covered with greaseproof paper to absorb any extra fat. Season with a pinch of sea salt. Continue until all are cooked.

For the Salsa di peperoncini, very finely chop the leaves and transfer to a bowl. Add the remaining ingredients, mix well and season to taste. The sauce has a kick.

With the hot fritters and the chilli salsa, a glass of ice cold Prosecco or something equally sparkling wouldn't go amiss!

Tip from the kitchen

Acqua fa ruggine: water makes you rust. Victor's Nonna Annunziata lived until she was 92 and swore by this. I'm not sure if it's true or if the sunshine of Italy naturally preserved her. She was tiny and very beautiful until her dying day.

CARPACCIO DI PESCE

Serves 2

½ small red onion

200g fresh halibut or sea trout

50g fresh dill, fronds only

50g fresh fennel herb, fronds only

20g capers in salt, rinsed

zest and juice of 1 unwaxed lemon

2 tbsp light Ligurian extra virgin olive oil, or Sofia's Olive Oil

sea salt flakes, to taste

We're famed in Scotland for our fresh fish and delicious smoked varieties. Victor's father's family, who came from Pozzuoli, love raw fish and shellfish of any variety. This simple carpaccio allows us to showcase Scotland's wonderful natural larder with some Italian panache.

Cut the red onion in half, slice it very, very finely, then soak it in cold water for about 5 minutes.

Very finely slice the fish into strips and layer on a platter. Chop the herbs finely and scatter on the fish. Sprinkle the sliced onion and the capers on top. Grate the zest of the lemon over the fish. Finish with the oil, lemon juice and a generous sprinkle of salt.

Chill in the fridge for about half an hour and serve.

Tip from the kitchen

Get to know your fishmonger – they can be your next best sous chef. For this recipe, ask them to debone a fillet of the fish but leave the skin on, as it will make it easier to thinly slice when you score against it.

MOZZARELLA IN CARROZZA
con Salsa di acciughe e pomodori

Makes one sandwich

½ small ball of mozzarella di bufala (scamorza is also delicious in this recipe)

2 good slices of fresh sourdough

1 free-range egg

2 tbsp milk

sea salt flakes and freshly milled black pepper, to taste

1 tbsp extra virgin olive oil

20g unsalted butter

For the Salsa di acciughe e pomodori

2 unsalted anchovies, finely chopped

2 sundried tomatoes, finely chopped

good pinch of dried oregano

small handful of fresh flat-leaf parsley, very finely chopped

small handful of fresh basil leaves, very finely chopped

1–2 dried chillies, crumbled into small pieces

2 tbsp extra virgin olive oil

sea salt flakes, to taste

If you're dreaming of eating pizza in Naples but a trip isn't on the horizon, and you've no time to make the pizza yourself, this is a quick fix. A TV supper super snack.

Salsa di acciughe e pomodori is a sophisticated sandwich spread. Using equal quantities of anchovies and sundried tomatoes gives you a depth and balance of great flavour, and neither one overpowers the other. It takes this simple dish to the next level.

First, make the Salsa di acciughe e pomodori. Mix all the ingredients together, check the seasoning and set aside.

Thinly slice the mozzarella and place it in a strainer for about 10 minutes, so the excess water drains off the cheese. Dry it with kitchen paper to remove any leftover liquid.

To assemble the sandwich, spread a generous spoonful of the sauce on one piece of bread. Layer the mozzarella on top and sandwich the slices of sourdough together. Beat the egg and milk, and season with salt and lots of black pepper.

Heat the oil and butter in a frying pan to coat the bread when frying. When it starts to foam, it's ready.

Dip both sides of the sandwich in the egg mixture, give it enough time to soak up the mixture, then fry until golden brown. The sandwich needs time to cook, so the cheese is hot and starting to melt. Lower the heat if you feel it's browning but not heating the filling all the way through.

Remove from the pan and place on some kitchen paper to soak up any excess butter. Serve cut in half and wrapped in some brown paper. Put some *Cafe Italia* music on and enjoy your city break on the couch with a glass of Cesanese.

Tip from the kitchen

If you can't have a holiday to Italy, watch *Three Coins in a Fountain* if you don't want to cry... or *Cinema Paradiso* or *Roman Holiday* if you do.

POLENTA CON FONTINA

Serves 2–3

For the polenta

750ml water

sea salt flakes, to taste

250g bramata polenta

200g greens, such as wild garlic, borage, spinach or scarola (an Italian frizze style lettuce

150–200g Fontina, grated (Asiago is slightly milder)

50g Parmigiano Reggiano, freshly grated

drizzle of light olive oil, to serve

Tip from the kitchen

Please don't use instant polenta. Be authentic and stick to the best ingredients. They taste so much better. If you have any leftover polenta, pour onto a plate and allow to cool. You can store this in the fridge for two or three days. To reheat, cut into slices and fry with some extra virgin olive oil until golden. This makes a delicious breakfast with a fried egg.

Polenta is a love or hate Marmite dish. It tends to be loved in cakes; it's amazing what sugar can do. For me, even with my love of sweet things, I prefer polenta when it is as savoury and as luscious as in this dish. In our house this says winter is coming.

One of my favourite cousins, Anita, came from Emilia-Romagna – Parmigiano country and a very different food region to ours. Polenta is as much at the heart of their cooking as ours, deep in the Lazio mountains. This recipe takes both families' traditions up a notch into the Valle d'Aosta territory in the Alps, home to the amazing unpasteurised cow's milk Fontina cheese.

First wash and coarsely chop the greens. Blanch in boiling, salted water. Reserve some of the cooking water before you drain the greens, then splash with cold water to stop the cooking process. Set them aside.

Some of the family like to fry the greens in garlic at this stage, but I prefer to keep it cheesy with no garlic. Up to you.

To make the polenta, choose a large heavy-bottomed pot, as it can stick. Add the water. Bring it to a simmer and season with salt. It's vital that you add enough salt, otherwise this can be a washout before you start. Hold the polenta in one hand and a long wooden spoon (a large balloon whisk works even better) in the other. Start stirring the water and then very slowly add the polenta in a very fine shower. If you get this first part of the mixing right, with no lumps, it makes cooking easier. Continue until all the polenta has been added. Mix for a few minutes to make sure there are no lumps and then lower the heat to as low as it will go, and simmer for about 30 minutes. Stir regularly to stop the polenta sticking. The polenta will be cooked when the colour changes from yellow crunchy to golden creamy.

Add the greens and the cheese, and check the seasoning. If the polenta is too thick, add a little of the greens' cooking water. You are looking for the consistency of soft porridge.

Serve in a soup bowl with more freshly grated Parmigiano and a drizzle of light olive oil, such as a Ligurian variety. Heaven.

POLPETTE

Serves 4

500g best quality beef mince

50g fresh parsley, finely chopped

1 free-range egg

100g breadcrumbs, freshly grated

1 onion, very finely grated

sea salt flakes and freshly milled black pepper, to taste

For the sugo

1 large whole onion, with the skin removed

4 x tin (400g) premium quality Italian plum tomatoes, blended

sea salt flakes, to taste

Meatballs – straight out of the era of the first *Godfather* film.

Some recipes work best when made in larger quantities and I always think this is one of them. These meatballs can be eaten with pasta, with polenta, my girls love them with a classic Risotto alla Milanese. Francis Ford Coppola's portrayal of the Sicilian Mafia, starring Brando, De Niro and Pacino, is regarded by many as one of the best films ever made. (Yes, there were three: Victor loved Part II and I love Part III, just for the music.) A horrendous part of Italy's history (past and present) but great acting.

In the scene in the film where they prepare this dish, red wine is used in the recipe, but I don't include it here. Given the content of the movie, maybe it's best not to follow the script.

To make the meatballs, in a large bowl mix all the ingredients together. Form into small balls the size of golf balls and set aside. I use plastic gloves for this.

To make the sugo, choose a heavy-based casserole pot and add some oil – enough to just cover the bottom – and fry the onion whole. When soft and lightly coloured, add the tomatoes. I rinse each tin of tomatoes with about a third of cold water and add this to the pot. Raise the heat a little.

When the tomato starts to boil, lower the heat and add the meatballs. A trick I learned from another cousin in Italy is that there is no need to fry the meatballs separately, or to even seal them; this only makes your sugo greasy. We just place them in the tomato, like putting a baby in a bath. Cover with a lid and roast in the oven at 220°C/425°F/Gas 7 for about 1½–2 hours. Check the seasoning at the end and remove the whole onion.

You'll know when the sauce is ready, as the outside of the sauce should change colour from an orange-red to a more silky golden red colour.

Tip from the kitchen

Never add salt to any tomato sugo until the end. The salt can make the tomatoes very bitter. Season at the end and your sauce will be super sweet.

PASTONE

Serves 6

3 x 100g fresh ricotta

100g Pecorino Romano, grated

8 large free-range eggs

200g smoked pancetta, cut into small cubes

2 sprigs of rosemary, leaves only, very finely chopped

bay leaf for the nonnas – a common ingredient from the grandmothers

sea salt flakes and freshly milled black pepper, to taste

unsalted butter, softened, for greasing

2 x 250g packets of ready-made puff pastry (pre-rolled is easier)

flour, for dusting

egg wash made from 1 egg, beaten with a tablespoon of cold water

Tip from the kitchen

Trust is a skill you learn. If you've been let down in the past, don't let that hold you back in the future. If you break the pie when you flip it, squash it back in. It will still taste lovely and you can try again the next time.

Pastone is a family staple. I always make this for No. 1 daughter when she comes home after travelling. Both my grandmothers made this and so did Victor's grandmothers. All were very different. This is the latest evolution that's been serving me well for decades.

In a large bowl, crumble the ricotta until it is loose, then lightly beat. Add the grated cheese. Break in the eggs and mix until they are incorporated. Add the pancetta, rosemary and bay leaf. Season with salt and a lot of freshly milled black pepper and mix well. Set aside.

Preheat the oven to 200°C/400°F/Gas 6 and grease a 30cm pie tin with the softened butter.

I feel two small packets of pastry tend to make this next step easier. One to line the bottom of the tin and one for the top of the pie. Roll the first sheet of pastry out on a large floured surface so you have enough to cover the bottom and sides of the tin. Line it, then place the filling inside. The second pastry sheet needs to be rolled big enough to generously drape over the filled tin. Wash the edge of the pastry around the rim with the egg wash, then place the second pastry sheet on top so that they stick. Trim the excess pastry from around the rim of the tin and then gently roll the edges of the pastry together, as if you were tucking and rolling as you go. You need the pie to be sealed, as you have to turn it over halfway through cooking so the bottom pastry cooks. Next take a knife and gently score the edges of the pie all the way round. Criss-cross a diamond pattern lightly on the top of the pie and pierce the pastry in two places to allow the steam to escape when it's cooking. Bake in a preheated oven for 25 minutes. The pie will start to colour. Reduce the heat to 180°C/350°F/Gas 4.

The trick is not to be fooled by the cooked pastry on the top of the pie. You really need to turn the pie over. I've mastered flipping this with lots of practice. First release the pie around the edges of the tin. Place a large chopping board or large flat plate, if you have one big enough, on top of the pie. Put your oven gloves on and hold the tin and the board together, on both sides, turn the pie over and sit it on the board. I'd recommend you flip it over the sink, as the egg mixture can still be runny and can end up all over you and the floor, and it will be hot so be careful.

Remove the tin from the pie and then gingerly slide the pie back into the tin. If you release the sides, it should come out clean. There may be some edges sticking out of the tin once you've turned it over and put it into the tin, so just gently push these back inside. You'll be surprised how raw the underside of the pie is. Bake for 10 minutes more. The pie will have a bounce to the touch, will look golden brown and will smell heavenly. Allow to cool for 10 minutes, then remove from the tin and allow to rest on a wire cooling rack. Leave for 15–20 minutes before cutting.

BRUSCHETTA

The first time we went to Tuscany with the children they were tiny. Nonna G came, too. We stayed up in the mountains in a hotel attached to a horse farm about 20km from Pisa. The horses were for riding but occasionally appeared on the grill menu. The children, as you can imagine, were slightly horrified. They wouldn't think twice now, but then it was a talking point at dinner. All was forgiven when thick slices of homemade bread that had been chargrilled until almost black and a bottle of the farm's extra virgin olive oil appeared on the table. Good bread and good oil are still their favourite snack.

The word bruschetta originates from a Roman word meaning 'to toast over coals'. The Tuscans are famous for serving this bread with their equally heroic and iconic olive oils, but the southern Italians have cracked the toppings. By the time you get to Campania, the tomato has taken over.

The most important part of bruschetta is the bread. You need a good sourdough or dense country-style loaf. It doesn't matter if it's a day old; this usually makes it better. Next, you need to be generous with how you slice the bread. Nothing thinner than 1.5cm will do. OK, next if you don't have a wood-fired oven or a charcoal grill, a ribbed cast-iron pan will do the trick. A frying pan will work too, so don't panic. What's compulsory is good extra virgin olive oil.

Heat the pan until it's very hot – so hot you would want to very quickly move your hand before you touched the surface, if you were checking to see if it had heated. If you add a little oil at this stage, it will smoke, but this helps get the chargrilled flavour.

Generously brush or pour some oil over the bread, and then place it oil-side down onto the pan. Brush or drizzle the other side of the bread with more oil. When the bread has turned to golden and there are signs of charring, flip over and cook the other side of the slice. As you remove it from the pan, drizzle over a little more oil. It needs to feel slightly soaked to have its luxury level met.

Have your toppings prepared in advance because you have to enjoy bruschetta hot. The following are some of our favourites.

Bruschetta all'aglio

The addition of garlic on bruschetta is very southern Italian. Cut a large clove of garlic in half. Leave the skin on the garlic so your fingers don't get too pungent. Rub the garlic over the hot bruschetta and drizzle with a generous amount of oil.

———

Bruschetta al pomodoro

Per bruschetta

100g ripe tomatoes (I love San Marzano plum tomatoes best; baby sweet Pachino tomatoes are messy but delicious)

1 tsp sea salt flakes (you'd be surprised how much salt the tomatoes soak up – they need it to bring out the flavour)

1 tsp dried oregano

½–1 tsp dried chilli flakes

4–6 fresh basil leaves, torn up

2 tbsp extra virgin olive oil

sea salt flakes and freshly milled black pepper, to taste

There is a little beach hut between the port and the town in Ischia Porto. Despite its humble abode, the setting and the snacking are off-the-scale sensational. Here they always add some home-grown dried chilli flakes and it gives the extra kick we southerners love.

Many of the houses around the corner from this part of the beach usually have a basket sitting in an open doorway with jars of dried salted capers or oregano. Nonna Olivia could never pass by without buying something and having a little chat with the other nonni who would be sitting podding some beans in the shade of the afternoon sun. Happy memories.

Chop the tomatoes, or if you are using San Marzano, slice thickly and place in a bowl. Add the other ingredients and mix together. Leave for about half an hour at room temperature and then dress on top of the bruschetta, finishing with another drizzle of oil, a pinch of salt and lots of fresh black pepper.

———

Bruschetta al pistacchio

100g fresh pistachios

½ garlic clove

2 tbsp extra virgin olive oil

zest and juice of 1 unwaxed lemon

100g Pecorino Toscano (this is a young fresh sheep's milk cheese), freshly grated

100g mascarpone

sea salt flakes and freshly milled black pepper, to taste

Don't spread this paste – it needs to be served thick.

Using a pestle and mortar, cream the pistachios and garlic with the oil. Add the lemon zest and juice. Combine to a smooth paste, then fold in the grated Pecorino and mascarpone, and then season.

Bruschetta con crema di baccalà mantecato

250g salt cod

milk, to cover

few black peppercorns

drizzle of extra virgin olive oil

handful of parsley, chopped

sprinkle of dried chilli

During lockdown Victor watched endless YouTube videos of how to get the perfect mantecato. We thought we'd never get back to Italy again. Thankfully we've been to Venice a few times since and this is as close to how most serve it there. The cod in Veneto is very lightly salted, not the old age version we tend to get here in Scotland.

Soak the salt cod in water as directed on page 34.

Place the rinsed cod in a pan and cover with milk. Add a few black peppercorns and gently simmer for 10–15 minutes until the cod starts to collapse. Cool slightly and then remove the cod from the milk. Keep the milk. Be careful when you clean the fish – remove any skin and bones; there can be lots.

In a pestle and mortar, cream the fish. It's best to do this while the cod is still warm but not hot. Add one to two tablespoons of the cooking milk to help emulsify the mixture. You're aiming for the texture of a firm pâté.

Slowly add the oil. A light extra virgin olive oil is best for this. You're aiming to break up all the strands of fish so it's beautifully soft. Fold in a little chopped parsley and crumble in a little dried chilli. Spread thickly on the hot bruschetta or a slice of soft bagette.

Tip from the kitchen

Don't feel guilty. I've found it's a Catholic thing that only some inherit. After several decades, I've decided on abstinence.

VENETO

Veneto is one of Italy's top wine-producing regions, particularly for white and sparkling wines. Prosecco, most famously, comes from the Valdobbiadene DOP in the northern part of Veneto. The landscape here – with vines and more vines, as far as the eye can see, like a ribbed blanket gently draped over the rolling steep hillsides – is truly beautiful across all the seasons. Even when the vines are groomed back to within an inch of their lives, dusted with snow, you know they are safe and good things will come later.

Many towns in the region are worth a visit: Padua, Treviso, Asiago, home to one of the most beautiful cow's milk cheeses, and for all you romantics we can't forget Verona. The most beautiful in the world for both Victor and I is Venice, the city at the heart of Veneto. Our first visit as a couple was in 1996 – young love – but it never loses its magic.

The Instagrammable-ness of Venice takes the city break into another league and in truth it is one of the only spoilers of international tourism (when you are an international tourist yourself). Every visitor wants every iconic image. Venice has these at every corner and every bridge, and there are a lot of both. Avoiding selfie sticks and 'moments in the making' can become hazardous – plus you are constantly surrounded by water.

Twenty-five years ago you could get lost in the winding canal lanes and dark alleys; the pre-Google Maps cloak-and-dagger world of Casanova felt very real but pleasantly exciting, especially after dark.

One time we got lost till two in the morning and divorce could have followed; there was no taxi to hail or phone to ring, and if I'd spotted anything with four legs and a tail I could have died on the spot. I was petrified.

In previous years we've relied on the crowded *vaporettos* to transport us in cramped discomfort from A to B, but Venice on foot is far more leisurely. The centre around St Mark's Square is shockingly exuberant, but you pay for the scenery. Prosecco flows too easily until you get the bill. At Caffè Florian, believed to be the oldest coffee shop in Italy, its pristine white-clad waiters deliver laden silver trays to tiny velvet booths around the arches of the square. Your favourite 1920s to 1950s five-piece band will be playing at 10 euros a cover – cheaper than seats at the Fenice, more comfortable, and you get a suntan with better nibbles. If you make time to stay and sip, not drink, it's worth it for a true spot of unadulterated, indulgent people-watching.

A favourite Venetian restaurant is Antiche Carampane. You'll struggle to find it. We are often the only tourists. The grandparents mill around. There you will find classic food: baccalà mantecato, fegato alla Veneziana, gran fritto misto with soft shell crabs fished from the lagoon a few hours before, zucchini fritti and wines to match, from all our favourite producers from Veneto.

A very famous *cicchetti* bar is tucked around the back of the Accademia. *Cicchetti* is a tradition in Venice of standing and enjoying some little slices of bread with fabulous toppings for lunch – far better than any combi deal that we've been lured into thinking is civilised in Britain. At Cantine del Vino già Schiavi there are no reservations, no tables, just the *cicchetti* of the Venetian dialect and a glass of something delicious. Go early and queue, and just enjoy the Venetian way of life.

APERITIVI

Mandorle Speziate

200g blanched almonds

1 tsp sea salt flakes

1 tsp fresh rosemary, leaves only, very finely chopped

1 tsp fresh thyme, leaves only, very finely chopped

1 tsp dried chilli flakes

1 tbsp extra virgin olive oil

Noci con Miele

200g shelled fresh walnuts

½ tsp ground cinnamon

¼ tsp ground cloves

¼ tsp ground mace

2 tbsp light honey

½ tbsp extra virgin olive oil

Contini olives

100g each of three varieties of olives (such as Taggiasche, Castelvetrano and Gaeta)

100g caper berries in brine

½ garlic clove, roasted and crushed (roasting takes away the harsh edge of raw garlic, which can be overpowering)

1 fresh red chilli, deseeded and thinly sliced

1 cooked Amalfi lemon, very finely sliced, seeds removed (see p. 176)

1 tbsp extra virgin olive oil

There are times that a meal isn't required, just some deliciously salty, moreish and indulgent snacks that will calm your appetite. It's usually while you're enjoying a little pre-dinner aperitivo that these snacks are most required. At Casa Contini we never need an excuse to enjoy a little Martini or Campari, or both, with added gin for a Negroni, Victor's favourite. Little snacks will tease your tummy (literally aperitivo means to open your stomach) for what delights lie ahead. Here are some of our favourite aperitivi nibbles.

Mandorle Speziate

Be warned: the chilli and salt in these spicy toasted almonds make you drink more.

Heat the almonds in a hot, large frying pan. When coloured but not browned, add the salt, herbs, chilli flakes and a drizzle of oil. Toss for a few minutes and then set aside.

Noci con Miele

These Venetian honey walnuts are delicious on their own or served with chunks of fresh Pecorino.

Mix all the ingredients together and transfer the nuts to a flat roasting tray. Bake in the oven at 180°C/350°F/Gas 4 for 15 minutes until golden. Remove from the oven and allow to cool slightly before you eat them.

Contini Olives

We serve taralli, which are crunchy Puglian biscuits, or a little bowl of olives for aperitivo at Contini George Street.

Mix all the ingredients together and refrigerate overnight to help the flavours combine. Serve at room temperature.

Tip from the kitchen

Always give the cook the first drink. A happy cook usually guarantees a delicious dish. Too many alcoholic drinks, however, can have side effects, for the cook and the cooking, so be warned.

ARANCINI

Serves 4

For the risotto

1 small onion, grated

25g butter

250g arborio rice

60ml white wine

600ml vegetable stock

150g mozzarella

50g Parmigiano Reggiano

3–4 sticks of fresh thyme, leaves only

sea salt flakes and freshly milled black pepper, to taste

100g seasoned plain flour

3 eggs, beaten

200g breadcrumbs

These always make me think of Sicily.

You can vary the filling. We serve ours with butter sugo (p. 79) and lots of freshly grated Parmigiano, but sometimes hot from the frying pan is what you need. Small chunks of mortadella and pieces of cheese such as Taleggio work beautifully. A teaspoon of chilled ragù mixed with a handful of frozen peas is a true Sicilian sensation.

Gently fry the onion in the butter until cooked. Add the rice and, when toasted, the white wine. Cook off the wine and then very slowly start adding the stock. The flavour of the stock is so important to give a great foundation to the arancini. The team makes a vegetable stock and adds the skin ends of the Parmigiano for extra flavour. Cook for about 30 minutes until al dente.

Add the cheeses and the leaves of the thyme. Check the seasoning. You can make the risotto any flavour you wish. Let your creativity have a little seasonal seasoning fun. A favourite at Contini George Street is grated courgette and sliced courgette flowers.

Transfer the risotto to a large tray to allow it to cool. When cold, start forming into balls. You can use an ice cream scoop to help you keep them all even.

Stuff as you wish, or have them without a filling.

Transfer to the fridge and, once the risotto is chilled, dip the arancini in the seasoned plain flour, then the beaten egg mixture and finally the breadcrumbs. Once breaded, return to the fridge to set until you are ready to eat them.

Cook the arancini in the same way as the Frittelle (p. 33), frying in small batches until golden brown and the filling is warmed through. You can enjoy them hot, at room temperature or they are delicious as a cold snack.

Tip from the kitchen

Be humble. There is nothing worse than being caught with a big head that doesn't fit in the room. I feel like my head has gotten smaller over the years, but it may just be that the door frames are wider. I hope it's the former.

Zuppe

MINESTRA
con Pesto alla Genovese

Serves 4

2 onions, finely chopped

2 large leeks, finely chopped

2 tbsp extra virgin olive oil

4 large fluffy potatoes, finely chopped

sea salt flakes and freshly milled black pepper, to taste

600ml boiling water

1 head of broccoli, finely chopped

4 courgettes, finely chopped

250g fresh peas (if you can get your hands on them), or French beans

150g barley or farro, washed

For the Pesto alla Genovese

1 garlic clove, peeled

pinch of sea salt flakes

50g pine kernels, very lightly toasted in a dry frying pan and then allowed to cool

4–5 tbsp extra virgin olive oil (a light Ligurian variety made with Taggiasche olives is best, so it doesn't overwhelm the basil)

250g basil leaves, leaves only

50g Pecorino Romano, finely grated

50g Parmigiano Reggiano, finely grated

Victor loves soup when he's been digging in the kitchen garden. Minestra is full of iron, so is a perfect recovery soup after an outdoor workout. It is traditional to add grains or pulses to this robust green dish – I've suggested farro or barley here.

Adding the fresh pesto gives this soup an Italian passport. The fresh lift of the basil, garlic and cheese flavours really enhances the soup. If you have some spare toasted pine kernels, you can add these as an extra for a little crunch.

Choose a pot that's large enough to hold all of the ingredients. Very finely chop the vegetables – you want them all the same size. Lightly fry the onions and the leeks. Add the potatoes, season and add the boiling water. Cook the potatoes for about 10 minutes, as these will take longer than the other vegetables. Add the remaining ingredients, stir and season again.

Simmer for about 30–40 minutes until the barley is cooked and remove from the heat.

Pesto alla Genovese

This is a Ligurian sauce, but like many things in Italy, ingredients have travelled to make it, with a mix of Parmigiano Reggiano and Pecorino Romano visiting from Emilia-Romagna and Lazio respectively. While it's traditionally served with pasta, a generous spoonful can add a real depth of flavour to most soups.

Using a pestle and mortar, cream the garlic with a pinch of salt. Add the pine kernels and loosen the mixture with a little olive oil. When the kernels are a paste, gradually add the basil leaves, rubbing and blending into the garlic mixture. When smooth, add the Pecorino and Parmigiano and a little more salt, if needed. Add more oil as required until you have a smooth mixture that is the consistency of soured cream.

Tip from the kitchen

To truly be called Pesto alla Genovese, one ingredient is essential. We're really lucky that occasionally, especially in late summer, we are able to buy Genovese basil (Basilico Genovese DOP) direct from Liguria. It smells like fancy perfume that you want to eat. Victor being Victor grows this variety in our polytunnel in the summer. It's not a huge harvest, but it's a fragrant one.

PASTA E FAGIOLI

Serves 4

500g dried cannellini or borlotti beans

1 whole onion, peeled

2 tbsp extra virgin olive oil

2 whole dried chillies

700ml passata

200g fresh Italian sausages, left whole, or 200g calabrese sausage cut into large chunks

200g ditalini pasta

Italy in a bowl. Like so many dishes, each region and indeed each family will have its own variation. Many will use Italian sausage, or lardo, to give more flavour, but it's not necessary. The trick is to use quality dried borlotti or cannellini beans.

Soak the beans in double the volume of cold water with a teaspoon of bicarbonate of soda overnight.

Rinse the beans and refresh with more cold water. Bring to the boil and then rinse the beans again. This removes any residual bicarbonate. In a casserole pot, cover again with double the volume of water and bring to a simmer, place the lid on top and transfer to the oven at 130°C/265°F/Gas 1–2 and cook for 3 hours until the beans are super soft. Set the beans in the cooking liquid aside.

Gently fry the whole onion in the oil in a large soup pot. Add the chillies to flavour the oil. Add the passata and rinse the jar with the same volume of cold water and add to the pot. Waste not, want not.

Add the sausages if you are using them, then the beans with about a quarter of the cooking liquid. Simmer for 45 mins to 1 hour until the beans start to collapse and the soup starts to thicken. Add the pasta and cook until al dente.

Tip from the kitchen

Tinned beans are great, but not for this recipe. You can use fresh beans, but they are so difficult to source in the UK, and the season is so short, don't even waste your time looking.

MINESTRONE

Serves 4

2 tbsp extra virgin olive oil

1 garlic clove

1 x tin (400g) Italian plum tomatoes

2 carrots, finely chopped

2 onions, finely chopped

2 sticks of celery, finely chopped

2 courgettes, finely chopped

2 peppers (one red, one yellow), finely chopped

1 small head of broccoli, finely chopped

1 small cauliflower, finely chopped

1 tsp dried oregano

1 litre cold water

sea salt flakes and freshly milled black pepper, to taste

160g short cut macaroni (optional)

Parmigiano Reggiano, grated, to serve

Minestrone is at the heart of *la cucina povera*, Italy's kitchen of the poor. Considering the Mediterranean diet has a reputation for being one of the healthiest in the world, there is a strong argument that the people may know best – poor in this context is a definition we can't always see the value in. Serving with a generous grating of fresh Parmigiano Reggiano makes it regal.

Chop all the vegetables to the same size. The smaller they are, the more elegant the soup.

Heat the oil in a large soup pot, add the whole clove of garlic and heat to release the flavours. Add the tin of tomatoes and squash them to make a smooth sauce. Cook for about 10 minutes until glossy. Add the vegetables and the oregano, with about 1 litre of water, and season with salt and pepper. Simmer for about 45 minutes. Add the macaroni and cook this in the soup. Serve with a generous grating of fresh Parmigiano Reggiano.

Tip from the kitchen

Every kitchen needs a big pot. A five-litre stock or pasta pot is the minimum you will need to cook for a family of four. Our pasta pot was our wedding gift. Thirty years later, it's still doing the job and, believe me, it's worked for its keep. God bless Marion and James Dickson, who bought it for us.

ZUPPE DI PESCE

Serves 4

500g lobster or langoustine (luxury ingredients, but worth it for a special occasion)

500g mussels or clams, cleaned and soaked in ice-cold water (see Tip from the kitchen, p. 113, for instructions)

250g monkfish or gurnard (the monkfish has no bones but is expensive; the gurnard is cheap but is full of bones. Both have depth of flavour, so your choice)

250g squid, cleaned and cut into thin rings; heads cut in quarters, if they are large

2 garlic cloves

2 tbsp extra virgin olive oil

2 good glugs of white wine

10–12 strands of saffron soaked in 250ml warm water

700ml passata, plus about 150ml of water to rinse the jar

100g fresh parsley, leaves only, finely chopped

sea salt flakes, to taste

Tip from the kitchen

Sometimes the best meals come by accident. Experimenting is good, but stick to some basic guidelines. Keep it seasonal. Always go with fresh. If you have integrity when choosing your ingredients, the end results, whatever the experiment, will taste good.

This soup can be fit for a queen or a fishwife, depending on the fish or shellfish you choose. The base is exactly the same. If you're using langoustine or lobster, the flavours from the shells and the saffron combine brilliantly and the soup has a heady fragrance. You just want to get a fabulous big chunk of fried bread to suck up the delicious sauce.

Choose as wide a pot as you have, but it needs to be deep enough to fit in all the fish. If the pot is too deep, the fish will get bruised and will break up.

First, prepare the fish. It's important that you are cutting the fish to roughly the same size so they cook evenly. For the lobster: remove the claw and crack it all the way around, but leave it attached to the flesh. This will make it easier to eat and will help it cook evenly. Next, cut the lobster lengthwise. Wash out and discard the head and brain membrane. Cut the tail into three or four pieces. Wash and set aside.

For the langoustine: it's important to clean the digestive passage by twisting the middle fin at the end of the tail. This should release the digestive vein that runs up the back of the prawn. Wash and set aside.

Cut the white fish into chunks that are slightly bigger than the lobster tail pieces, as you don't want them to disintegrate when cooking. Clean the squid and cut into thin rings; cut the heads into quarters, if large.

You're now ready to start. Heat the garlic in the oil and cook until golden but not brown. Add the white wine and reduce by half. Add the saffron and liquid. Add the passata and the water and cook for about 10 minutes. The water just thins the tomato enough to make a sauce rather than a stew consistency. Cook for another 10 minutes.

Add the lobster claws, as these will take the longest to cook. Simmer gently for about 3 or 4 minutes. Turn the claws so they cook on the other side. Then gently place the fish and squid into the pan, then the mussels and lobsters or prawns on top. Cover with a lid and simmer very gently for 5 minutes until the mussels have opened. The fish and shellfish will have also cooked by then. Add the finely chopped parsley and check the seasoning.

CREMA DI POMODORO

Serves 4

1kg ripe fresh tomatoes, plum or stem varieties are best

100g unsalted butter

2 tbsp extra virgin olive oil

400g onions, peeled and chopped

4 celery sticks, very finely chopped

sea salt flakes, to taste

1 tsp caster sugar

1 litre stock (hot ham is my favourite, but water or vegetable stock works too)

8-10 basil leaves

sea salt flakes and freshly milled black pepper, to taste

100ml double cream

Growing up in the 1970s had many benefits, but while there was in my life an abundance of love and sweeties (how could there not be, living above an ice-cream shop?), I never remember an abundance of fresh fruit or vegetables. Don't get me wrong, they were there – but in moderation, within a balanced, healthy diet deemed appropriate for its day. The thought of making tomato soup with only fresh tomatoes would have been a luxury beyond our dreams. This soup always feels like a treat to me.

Blanch the tomatoes in boiling water and remove the skins. Roughly chop the tomatoes and set aside. Choose a heavy-bottomed soup pot and melt the butter and oil. Gently fry the onion and celery until very soft, but don't let them brown. Add the tomatoes and season with salt, then add the sugar. Next add the hot stock, then cover and simmer for about 30–40 minutes until the tomatoes have collapsed and the soup has started to thicken. Add the basil leaves. The heat of the soup is enough to release the aromas from the herb. You don't need to cook them any longer.

Either pass the soup through a mouli or blend. There are always some stalky parts from either the tomatoes or the celery, so if you have the patience to sieve the soup it's always worth it. Finally check the seasoning and add the cream. Heat just enough so the soup is hot, but you don't want to boil the cream.

Tip from the kitchen

Don't be a martyr – you'll be the only one to suffer.

CREMA DI FUNGHI
con Burro all'aglio

Serves 4

100g unsalted butter

2 tbsp extra virgin olive oil

400g onions, peeled and chopped

2 leeks, tough green shoots removed, very finely chopped

1kg Paris Brown mushrooms, washed and sliced

sea salt flakes and freshly milled black pepper, to taste

2 or 3 dried porcini, soaked in warm water (optional)

1 litre hot stock (chicken is my favourite but water works too)

8-10 parsley leaves

100ml double cream

1 tbsp garlic butter (see recipe below)

For the Burro all'aglio

1-2 garlic cloves, depending on your preference, sliced

50g fresh parsley, leaves only, finely chopped

1 fresh red chilli, seeds removed, chopped

50g unsalted butter

pinch of sea salt flakes

This recipe works for any variety of mushrooms. If you're lucky and have an expert forager in the family, the humble Paris Brown or button mushroom is lifted to superhero status when bulked out with fresh porcini. If you don't have the luxury of a forager, and you don't have any dried porcini, add the garlic butter to give an extra surprise.

Choose a heavy-bottomed soup pot and melt the butter and oil. Gently fry the onions and leeks until very soft, but don't let them brown. Add the mushrooms and season with salt and pepper. It's really important to sweat down the mushrooms until they are super soft and cooked. This helps to deepen the mushroom flavour. If you have some dried porcini, you can add them at this point. Make sure you rinse them well, as there can be residual grit in the mushrooms and in the water you've soaked them in. Strain the water and add to the pot.

Next add the stock, then cover and simmer for about 30–40 minutes until the mushrooms are cooked and the soup has started to thicken. Add the parsley leaves.

Whizz the soup in a blender until smooth. Victor likes a little texture but choose whichever consistency you prefer. Finally check the seasoning and add the cream. Serve with a drizzle of melted garlic butter.

Burro all'aglio

This is a very useful flavour to have in your arsenal. It can be served with a lovely grilled steak or a piece of fish; it is great melted over steamed vegetables and, of course, it's wonderful for garlic bread, which isn't Italian at all but totally moreish and a family guilty pleasure.

Place the garlic and parsley in a pan with the chilli, butter and a pinch of salt, and allow it to melt. Add a few teaspoons of the warm butter when serving the soup.

Tip from the kitchen

The base for Burro all'aglio, with the added juice and zest of a lemon, is excellent when cooking shellfish.

ZUPPE DI LENTICCHIE
con Battuto di lardo

Serves 4

1 tbsp extra virgin olive oil

2 onions, very finely chopped

2 carrots, very finely chopped

1 small fennel, very finely chopped

2 celery sticks, very finely chopped

500g brown Castelluccio lentils, rinsed well

2 fresh or cured Italian sausages (skin removed from the cured sausage)

2 large potatoes, peeled and finely diced

1 litre vegetable stock or boiling water

Scottish red lentil soup made with a ham hock and this Italian brown lentil soup are friends as well as relatives. There are so many traditions and similarities in them, but the tastes couldn't be more different.

Gently melt one or two tablespoons of Battuto di lardo into the pot of soup before serving. This release of flavour gives an earthy finish to the dish. It says I'm a bowl of Italian goodness, for sure.

Choose a large soup pot for this. Add the oil and gently sweat the onions, carrots, fennel and celery until soft but not brown. Add the lentils, sausage and potatoes. Cover with the hot stock or water and simmer very gently for 1½ hours, until the lentils are soft and all the vegetables are cooked. Remove the sausages, slice them and add them back into the soup.

Battuto di lardo

This is the tradition of creaming a few thin slices of lardo with a little salt, rosemary or dried chilli in a pestle and mortar until it's creamy. It's then added to a stew or soup. Occasionally I'll add a little fresh garlic. There are times when your immune system needs a reboot and this will do it, guaranteed. Try it – it's delicious, but pungent. It will keep in the fridge.

Tip from the kitchen

Lardo di Colonnata is the most famous Tuscan cured fat made from the older pigs. It can be eaten thinly sliced or used in cooking like bacon, or as in this recipe gently melted to release its juicy flavour.

BRODO

Per person

3–4 ladles of chicken stock (see instructions below)

1–2 nests of vermicelli pasta

1 egg

squeeze of lemon

50g Parmigiano Reggiano

small bunch of flat-leaf parsley

Chicken stock

Makes approx. 1 litre

12 chicken wings or 6 thighs

2 litres cold water

generous pinch of salt

3 celery sticks, halved

1 large bunch of flat-leaf parsley

Tip from the kitchen

Medicine soup works. Salt is good, just saying. Fat is good. Just saying, too.

We have roast chicken most Sundays. My frugal side spatchcocks the chicken and uses the salvaged backbone of the carcass with the giblets and any trimmings from the wings or a leg to make a mini pot of broth that will feed us one day during the week – as a bowl of soup, a stock for risotto or, another family favourite, a curry. For a decent pot of broth, you'll need a decent amount of chicken. A boiling fowl is a treasure if you can get your hands on one. My children call this broth 'medicine soup'. It always works a trick when they're not feeling at their best.

———

Chicken stock can be very fatty, so I recommend making it a day in advance. I used to wash the chicken, but we're now told not to do so.

Place the chicken pieces in a 2 litre stock pot. Cover with cold water, add the salt and bring to the boil. Reduce to a simmer and skim off the foam that comes to the surface. It will take 5–10 minutes of skimming and simmering until the broth clears. Taste. You may need to add a little more salt.

Add the celery and parsley, and half cover the pot with a lid. Simmer for 2–2½ hours. I put my pot with the lid closed in the roasting oven and cook for the same time. It works just as well and the house doesn't get all steamed up.

Strain the broth into a jug, leave to cool and refrigerate overnight. When the stock solidifies, the fat will rise to the surface. Remove with a spoon.

It's better to strain the stock while the chicken is hot, as this way you can remove any flesh from the bones or carcass and save this to add to the soup. Discard the rest.

———

For a bowl of brodo, take 3–4 ladles of stock and heat in a small saucepan. In a separate pan of boiling salted water, crush 1–2 nests of vermicelli pasta and simmer for about 2–3 minutes until al dente. Drain and add to the broth.

Beat the egg, lemon juice, cheese and parsley together, and drizzle into the hot broth. Steam for 2–3 minutes until cooked.

BRODO DI CARNE

Serves 4

For the brodo

250g piece boiling beef

250g spale bone

2–3 tsp salt

2 carrots, peeled and left whole

2 leeks, trimmed and washed thoroughly, left whole

2 sticks of celery, left whole

1 x tin (400g) plum tomatoes

200g pastina

For the main meal

1 garlic clove, sliced

small handful of fresh parsley leaves, roughly chopped

20g baby capers in salt, rinsed to remove the salt

1 dried chilli, crushed

2 tbsp extra virgin olive oil

1 tbsp red wine vinegar

pinch of sea salt flakes

Tip from the kitchen

You really need to get to know your butcher. The cuts of beef you need for this are the cheapest and often won't even appear on a butcher's counter.

This is a winter staple. At Casa Contini we call it beef broth, after Nonna Olivia's name for this soup. If chicken brodo is the start of the recovery, beef brodo is the final stage of returning to full health. It can be just a soup or a soup plus a main course, with all the nutrition you need.

———

Start with the brodo. Place the meat in a large pot and cover with cold water. Add 2–3 teaspoons of salt and bring the water to the boil. You need to be able to taste the salt in the water. Reduce to a simmer and remove any of the residual foam that comes to the surface. Once the water starts to look clear, add the whole vegetables and the tin of tomatoes. Squash the tomatoes lightly and always rinse the tin with cold water and add to the pot to get all the flavour.

Cover with a lid and put the pot, with the lid closed, in the roasting oven at 220°C/425°F/Gas 7 for 2–2½ hours. Don't be afraid to overcook the broth. The longer you cook it, the more intense the flavours are and the more tender the beef is.

When ready, take out the vegetables and the meat and set aside. You can use these for the main meal (see below).

Serve the hot broth with pastina. These tiny pieces of dried pasta come in many different shapes, from riso and orzo to the little letters that we always gave the children. Cook the pastina separately and add into the strained broth.

———

The beauty of this is that the strained broth can be the first course, and then the boiled vegetables, with some extra steamed beans or broccoli, and the marinated meat combine to make a perfectly balanced, healthy and relatively good value dinner for a family.

Remove any meat from the boiling beef bone. Make sure you remove any sinew. Place the meat on a serving dish. Slice the spale bone, removing any excess fat, and add that to the plate.

Slice the garlic over the meat and dress with the parsley, capers and chilli, and the oil, vinegar and salt.

TUSCANY

The image of a Tuscan farmhouse, its driveway lined with cypress trees and rolling vineyards flanking all around, captures the idea of Italian luxury. The villa in *Succession* is currently distracting me . . .

Towns such as San Gimignano, with its 72 towers, or Pisa, with the steal-the-show leaning version, or Siena, Lucca and (how can we forget) Florence, make Tuscany a winning region.

Its olive oils are prized as the best in Italy, perhaps the world. Chianti, Brunello di Montalcino, Vino Nobile di Montepulciano – the ultimate who's who of aspirational wine luxury – are all from here.

Tuscany really is a showstopper. If the wine leaves your senses bombarded, then Florence leaves you needing treatment. Stendhal syndrome, or Florence syndrome, is when you are left feeling

faint, confused, with a rapid heartbeat, and you may even get hallucinations as the wonders around you leave you stunned.

I've never suffered the effects of this syndrome. Venice or Rome will always be my first

choices, but Florence, with its architecture and its art, is almost excessive. I suppose it's hard to say you don't like rubies when there are diamonds and sapphires to choose. Italy spoils you with everything, from food to music, fashion to architecture, and Florence does have everything: Michelangelo's *David*, housed in the Accademia Gallery; Ponte Vecchio; *The Birth of Venus* by Botticelli, on every tourist's checklist, housed in the Uffizi. The Duomo and Baptistery are extras not to be forgotten, if you even could. La Giostra, in classic trattoria style, surrounds you with images of the world's great and good.

One year we stayed in Viareggio, a 1920s seaside town on the Tuscan coast, and took a bus trip to Florence. Victor chose to 'forget' his credit cards. He ordered a Fiorentina, the T-bone steak of the region, with new season porcini. His two favourite things but definitely not mine. This lunch cost all our money. We didn't even have enough change for a gelato. Perhaps this is the real source of why I don't love Florence.

If you've had lunch, the next best thing to do in Florence is digest in the Boboli Gardens. They are vast and offer another fabulous cooling 'Statue of Neptune' fountain. On another occasion, no steak involved, Victor and I lost a most romantic day without the children in this very spot. Florence came good.

Siena is another great destination in Tuscany. Home to the Palio, which has been held in this venue since 1659. Tickets are impossible to get hold of for a race that lasts seconds, not even minutes. The things not to miss are the colours of the riders, the livery of the horses and the matching flags that adorn the houses.

Siena is in the middle of the Italian countryside. Warning: don't order fish (Nonna G ordered lobster); it will cost more than a Fiorentina.

CECI E PATATE
con Olio al rosmarino

Serves 4

500g dried chickpeas, soaked in cold water overnight with a teaspoon of bicarbonate of soda

2 medium onions, very finely chopped

125g pancetta affumicata, chopped (optional)

2–3 dried chillies

1–2 large fluffy potatoes, diced

1 tbsp extra virgin olive oil

sea salt flakes and freshly milled black pepper, to taste

For the Olio al rosmarino

2–3 tbsp extra virgin olive oil

1 sprig of fresh rosemary, leaves only, very finely chopped

1 garlic clove

This Tuscan soup almost feels medieval, but is sophisticated in its flavour.

Pulses are used all over Italy. The tradition of storing cured and dried food in the larder for sustenance over the winter months is thankfully still in practice today. I don't do much preserving myself, as we are fortunate to have such a great supply of fresh food all year round, but dried and tinned foods are key in my cupboards. Dried chickpeas have a beautiful earthy flavour but are remarkably light, and with our weather in Scotland they won't go amiss at any time of the year.

Drain the chickpeas and rinse, then cover with double the volume of fresh water. Bring to the boil and then drain and rinse again. Cover the chickpeas again with double the volume of water and then bake in a slow oven (130°C/265°F/Gas 1–2) for 4 hours until they are soft and very tender.

In a large soup pot, gently fry the onions until super soft but not browned. Add the pancetta, if using, and fry until golden. Add the chillies and potatoes, and the cooked chickpeas. Add just enough of the cooking liquid to cover the ingredients – you don't want a watery soup. You can add boiling water to top up, if required.

Season with salt and freshly milled black pepper. Simmer for about 20–30 minutes until the potatoes are super soft and starting to collapse. Check the seasoning and then add a dash of Olio al rosmarino.

Olio al rosmarino

There are many Italian recipes that rely on only a few ingredients. Sometimes a little extra, like this oil, can make all the difference.

Heat the extra virgin olive oil with rosemary and a whole clove of garlic in a pan. When the garlic has started to brown, drain the oil into the soup.

Tip from the kitchen

Be very careful if you try to make this soup and then reheat for another day. The consistency is so thick that it will stick to the bottom of the pot and can burn really easily.

Pasta

HOMEMADE PASTA

Per person

approx. 100g pasta flour

1 large, free-range egg

no salt or olive oil is required

Nonna Olivia would often use duck eggs. At Casa Contini and in the restaurant, we follow this recipe with hens' eggs for cut pasta, sheets or shapes, like ravioli or tortelloni. You'll need a pasta machine.

Weigh the flour in a large bowl and form a well in the middle. Crack the egg into the well and gently start to mix together. You can use a fork, your fingers or a mixer, if it's strong enough – mine isn't. We always do this part by hand.

As the dough starts to combine, transfer it to a floured surface and the hard work begins. At home we'll make from six up to 20 eggs' worth of pasta, depending on the occasion. It will take at least 20 minutes to knead to stretch the gluten, making the dough silky smooth, so that when you run your finger over the surface it doesn't ripple. The texture changes as you knead the dough, so give it the extra elbow grease in order that it's mixed and prepared for the next part of the task. Cover with cling film and leave to rest in the fridge for 1 hour.

When you start to roll out the pasta, the dough should be at room temperature. The golden rule is only ever to turn the pasta handle clockwise. If you turn it the wrong way, you will break the machine.

Cut a bread-sized slice of dough. Flatten it with your fingers and then start to roll it out with the pasta machine. The trick is to ensure the dough is dry enough so that you need very little, if any, additional flour when rolling. Start on the widest setting.

This takes time and you need to fold and roll, fold and roll until the dough slides comfortably through the rollers. You're working towards a wide but long sheet of pasta. Reduce the roller setting a notch at a time. The finest setting can be too fine, depending on the type of machine. Use your instinct.

Once all the dough has been rolled into long flat sheets, you can start cutting or shaping. For fresh tagliarini, use the narrow setting, or for tagliatelle, use the wider setting. If you're making lasagne or filling pasta for ravioli, sometimes it's better to have a slightly thicker pasta sheet. This comes down to your confidence and practice.

Tip from the kitchen

Don't throw away the end of the Parmigiano. Give it a wash and add it to a slow-cooked pot of stock or soup. It provides a lovely added extra flavour that you didn't expect.

Have long sheets of baking parchment on your kitchen surface or dining-room table for when you start to cut the sheets into shapes. Place the rolled, cut pasta directly onto the paper. Try not to touch it too much, as that's what makes it stick together.

Cook from fresh or leave to dry overnight.

When it's time to cook the pasta, choose your biggest pot and fill it with boiling, salted water. The parchment can go directly into the water if the pasta is slightly stuck to it, as the strands will immediately release. Cook until the water returns to the boil and simmer for a minute. Drain and drown in delicious sugo.

PASTA AL POMODORO

Allow 80g of pasta per person

Pomodoro fresco

Per person

200g ripe Italian Pachino cherry tomatoes, washed and cut in half

1 garlic clove, peeled and sliced

3–4 tbsp extra virgin olive oil

pinch of sea salt flakes

handful of fresh basil leaves

Butter sugo

Serves 2–3

2 x tin (400g) Italian plum tomatoes, liquidised

1 large shallot, peeled but not chopped

125g unsalted butter

1 tsp caster sugar

This is a staple. There are many ways to cook the tomato sauce, or sugo. It can be rich and indulgent, or fresh and light. Here are the basics.

Pomodoro fresco

Served with spaghettini, this is a Neapolitan classic.

Add the tomatoes, garlic and half the oil to a large frying pan and increase the heat. It will take the same time to cook as any quality dried spaghettini. Add more oil as the sugo cooks to help emulsify the tomatoes, as they start to separate and break down. Season with salt and add the basil. When the pasta is cooked, drain and toss it together with this very light, very tasty and most Neapolitan sauce.

Butter sugo

This is a staple in my kitchen at home and at Contini George Street. A Marcella Hazan classic, it's as northern as they come, thanks to the use of butter rather than olive oil. It's brilliant with gnocchi or homemade pasta.

Add the tomatoes, whole shallot, butter and sugar to a cast-iron casserole. Rinse the tins by half-filling with cold water and add to the tomatoes. Bring to the boil, stir, then reduce the heat to the lowest level.

Balance the lid of the pot on top of a wooden spoon left lying part of the way across the pot. This allows the sugo to slowly thicken and concentrate. Simmer for about 35–40 minutes.

The sugo is ready when you see it reducing around the edge and the colour changing to a glossy red tone.

Sugo con carne

Sugo con carne

Serves 6

1 large onion, skin removed

2 tbsp extra virgin olive oil

500g piece of pork chop (or fillet steak, if it's Christmas Day)

8 x tin (400g) Italian plum tomatoes, liquidised

1 cured Italian sausage, skin removed and cut into pieces

2 whole dried chillies

sea salt flakes and freshly milled black pepper, to taste

This is the sugo we make for homemade pasta. It's the sugo that makes me think of Ciociaria. It's rich and luscious, but be warned: fresh pasta drinks sauce. The same recipe works great with oxtail instead of the other meats.

A chunky pasta like rigatoni or millerighe works with this sugo. The ribs on this thick, chunky, 'sock'-shaped pasta, named after my Nonna Marietta's knitting, soak up the sauce. She loved knitting the leg part but didn't like turning the heels.

Gently fry the whole onion in oil in a large cast-iron casserole until golden. Lightly brown the meat, but not the sausage. Add the tomatoes (rinse the tins by half filling with water and add this to the sauce too). Slowly bring to a simmer. Add the sausage now and the chillies.

Bring to the boil. Stir and then cover with the lid and bake in the oven at 220°C/425°F/Gas 7 for 2½ hours. The sugo is ready when you see it reducing around the edge, and fats and juices from the meat are bubbling on the surface.

Check for seasoning at the very end. Never season until after it's cooked.

Tip from the kitchen

I'm a whole onion girl. Some of the family chop the onion for the sugo, but I really don't think it adds anything other than the texture of oily onion.

PASTA AI PEPERONI

Allow 80g of pasta per person

Serves 2

1kg red and yellow peppers

4 tbsp extra virgin olive oil

1 small garlic clove, peeled and sliced

100g Taggiasche olives, stones removed and cut in half

handful of capers in salt, rinsed to remove the salt

sea salt flakes and freshly milled black pepper, to taste

12–18 fresh basil leaves, torn in half

There are a few stages to this dish and you can't cut them out. There are also very few ingredients. This is a summer pasta in our house. I make this dish using dried casareccia pasta.

Start by roasting the peppers whole on a baking sheet at 200°C/400°F/Gas 6 for 40 minutes until the skins are black and blistered. The next job is to remove the skin and seeds from the peppers. Pierce the peppers to release any extra juices. Set these juices aside in the bowl you'll be putting the cleaned peppers into.

Place a pepper on a clean board and gently remove the blistered skin: you need to remove all of this; if you don't, it will make the sauce bitter. Next, cut the pepper in half, remove the stalk and scrape out all the seeds. Chop the pepper into small, thin, finger-sized pieces and transfer to the bowl. Continue until all the peppers are prepared.

Boil the pasta in salted water.

Start making the sauce. I use a large, flat frying pan for this. Add the oil and gently cook the garlic, but don't let it colour. Add the peppers and a few tablespoons of the reserved juices. Add the olives and capers, and check the seasoning. Don't be shy to add extra olive oil.

While the pasta is cooking, add the basil to the sauce, so it doesn't discolour and the aroma is even more intense. Drain the pasta and mix into the sauce, adding a tablespoon of the reserved cooking water, then simmer for a few minutes until combined.

Tip from the kitchen

Peperoni are capsicums, the pepper vegetable; they are not spicy cured sausages. Fake food fact. That sounds a bit angry, but it's not meant to be. Honest.

BROCCOLETTI

Allow 80g of pasta per person

Serves 2

200g broccoli or broccoli spears

3–4 tbsp extra virgin olive oil

2 large garlic cloves, peeled and sliced

2–3 dried chillies, crushed

sea salt flakes and freshly milled black pepper, to taste

100g ricotta salata, grated, to serve

Victor and I almost separated when I cooked a selection of three different pasta shapes with a sauce I had in the fridge on a 'use up Monday'. He felt I was breaking the unwritten Italian constitution of always serving the correct pasta with the correct sauce. I was just in 'get everyone fed' mode. It really is all about shape and sauce compatibility, though. We didn't separate, but I haven't used a selection of pasta in the same meal since.

Long dried pasta, like spaghetti or linguine, works really well for this recipe, but one of the best shapes is the Puglian pasta orecchiette ('little ears'), as it acts like a little bucket to hold in all the flavour.

An additional ingredient can be a fresh Italian sausage, if you're having a 'use up Monday' moment, too. Remove the skin from the raw sausage and fry it in the oil until it's all broken up and cooked, then carry on as below.

Cut up the broccoli, including any leaves or stalks, so they will fit into the pasta when it's cooked. Blanch in salted water and drain.

Start cooking the pasta: most varieties of orecchiette take about 10–15 minutes to cook, so check the instructions.

Choose a large frying pan and gently warm the oil with the sliced garlic and crushed chillies. You don't want the garlic to burn but you want it golden, so the flavours are released.

Add the blanched broccoli to the oil and heat through. Add more oil if you think it looks dry. Season with salt and freshly milled black pepper. Nonna Olivia always cooked the broccoli until it was very soft, and when she fried it, it fell apart and became a sauce. I tend to leave it slightly al dente, but either way works.

Add the pasta when ready.

Try with grated ricotta salata, a Puglian delight, which has an almost stringy texture.

Tip from the kitchen

Pastasciutta is the name for any factory-made dried pasta using durum wheat. The quality varies, like any other food. The best are slow grain, slow-dried varieties. Many use commercially grown grains and are fast-dried in huge bulk. The most famous are bronze die (referring to the plates that cut the pasta) and come from Gragnano. They say their water is best, so their grain is best. There is a time and place for fresh and dried pasta – choose wisely.

SPAGHETTI CON TONNO

Allow 80g of pasta per person

Serves 2

1 garlic clove, sliced

2 dried chillies, crushed

1 tbsp extra virgin olive oil

1 x tin (400g) Italian plum tomatoes, liquidised

50g capers in salt, rinsed

1 x tin (250g) tuna in brine, drained

25g fresh parsley leaves, finely chopped

sea salt flakes and freshly milled black pepper, to taste

Spaghetti alle vongole, or pasta with clams, is a dish we all love. It's food you eat as close to the beach as possible, or on it, if you're lucky. *Vongole veraci*, tiny little clams the size of your thumbnail, are only available in the Mediterranean. Steam them with olive oil, garlic, chilli and parsley. To prepare the dish authentically, you finish cooking the pasta with the clams in the saucepan. Add the drained very al dente pasta and a little extra of the pasta water – cooking the pasta with the pasta water emulsifies the starch and the sauce becomes creamy and buttery.

Alas, I've never found these clams in Scotland (and surf clams can be slightly chewy and need to be soaked, as they are full of sand). So, an alternative is this dish. It has fed us hundreds of times in a hunger emergency. Think of it as the ultimate store cupboard fast food. I make this dish with linguine.

Choose a large frying pan and gently heat the garlic and chilli in the oil. Add the tomatoes and bring to the heat.

Add the capers and tuna, and allow to simmer for about 10 minutes until the sauce is sticky and cooked. Add the parsley and check seasoning.

Boil the pasta and, when al dente, drain and add to the sauce. Keep a little of the pasta water, if case you need to loosen the sugo.

Tip from the kitchen

Supermarkets will often sell tinned tomatoes flavoured with herbs. Stay away. Choose an ethical brand of San Marzano (we always use Mutti) and you'll not be disappointed.

LAZIO

When we visit our home, I Ciacca, we usually fly into Rome, the jewel of the region of Lazio. If you asked Nonna G what she loves about the Eternal City, the answer would be the Vatican. I'm more drawn to Via Condotti, the famous shopping street that leads from the Spanish Steps.

In Rome, the old and the ancient cross paths constantly. We've dined in many restaurants where the patrons have escorted us to hidden rooms that descend through centuries to reveal moments of another time. Food and history are our markers.

Giolitti, the ice-cream emporium, is located close to the Pantheon, the best preserved structure from the classical era and the largest dome in the world for more than a thousand years.

Sant' Eustachio, the church itself and the district just behind, undoubtedly boasts Rome's, if not the world's, best coffee shop. Made behind a screen, in a jam-packed bar, their cappuccino is an experience we never miss.

For more refined and relaxing sites, the Campo de' Fiori early morning market is visually and aromatically exhilarating. Its iconic La Carbonara restaurant serves excellent Carbonara. Or Osteria da Fortunata, a tourist spot to watch the cook twisting fresh sciavatelli pasta all day long in the window, will feed you well, if remarkably quickly. Bernini's Piazza Navona is a favourite relaxation point.

Early starts in Rome are essential. There is always too much not to miss, and lunch will inevitably distract you for a couple of hours. Ristorante Piperno never disappoints. A hotel concierge recommended this restaurant to us years ago. Once we dined in July and a summer shower poured down on us. We were outside under a huge parasol. We are always reluctant to move

inside, so the lovely waiter, Franco, served us every dish under an umbrella. Beautiful, fun, happy tummy memories.

We've lost hours walking in Rome and I wouldn't ask for one moment back. I love the carefree *passeggiata* – having time to squander is one of life's luxuries, best enjoyed in Rome.

I feel very lucky that I've been able to share great travel journeys with Victor and the children. Photos early morning on Via del Corso with a gladiator or in the evening at the Trevi Fountain with gelato are in many a scrapbook. Funnily enough, there are probably more photos of Bucatini all'Amatriciana, Saltimbocca, Carciofi alla Giudia and Bomboloni than our children. I'm sure the kids are there somewhere . . .

GNOCCHI CACIO E PEPE

Serves 4

For the gnocchi

500g fluffy potatoes, such as Maris Piper

plain flour (not a pasta or bread flour, as this is too heavy)

For the Cacio e pepe
Per person

50g unsalted butter

50g Pecorino Romano, finely grated, plus extra to sprinkle on top

25g Parmigiano Reggiano, finely grated

freshly milled black pepper, to taste

pinch of sea salt flakes

At Contini George Street, our two top sauces for gnocchi are butter sugo finished with mozzarella di bufala (classic Gnocchi alla Sorrentina), and Cacio e pepe.

Cacio e pepe is a Roman dish whose name translates as 'Cheese and pepper'. Yes, cheese and pepper only, because something so very beautiful doesn't need to be tarted up. Fresh, simple cooking is the heart of the best Italian kitchen.

This recipe is the result of hundreds of years of 'women's' work (no offence intended to any man) and I feel in this instant the job is finally done. This is the best gnocchi recipe for now and for ever.

My maternal grandmother, paternal grandmother, Victor's paternal grandmother and his maternal grandmother were all born within 20 miles of each other. They all made gnocchi but all had a different recipe. One added an egg, while some added salt and another added self-raising flour. The degrees of difference in texture and density had to be tasted to understand what indigestion was.

This recipe has been tried and tested over the years of my married life and it's safe to be handed down to the next generation without any further tweaks – regardless of any new grandmothers-in-law who may be added to the mix. It's also the recipe we use every day in Contini George Street, so you're in safe hands there too.

Peel and cut the potatoes into quarters and place in a large pot. Cover with cold water and simmer until tender. They need to be soft. Do not add salt to the water.

Drain and leave the potatoes in the colander, sitting over the pot, and cover with a clean towel.

While the potatoes are still warm, mash them until light and fluffy. Weigh the potatoes and then add half the weight of plain flour and mix well. I usually do this first stage in the pot in the sink, as it makes less mess.

Transfer to a clean surface and slowly knead. The mixture will take about 4–5 minutes to be incorporated. It needs to be bound together. It's not as firm as a bread mixture, so you can be light with your hands, but it needs to be well mixed.

Tip from the kitchen

Never add salt to your water when you're cooking the potatoes. It will make them hard and heavy. You only need to salt the water when you're cooking the gnocchi.

Roll out the mixture to about 1cm thick and then cut into 1cm strips. Cut into 1cm cubes and then press with a fork to slightly squash and turn the dumplings.

Once cut, lay on top of sheets of greaseproof paper. There is no need to dust the paper with any additional flour. They can sit for up to 4 hours in a cool kitchen without discolouring, but don't put them in the fridge.

Next, cook the gnocchi in a large pot of boiling salted water. Gently stir and cover with the lid until the water returns to the boil. Simmer for another minute or two until cooked through.

For the sauce, melt the butter in a large frying pan until soft and gently bubbling. Add the cheese and lots of freshly milled black pepper.

Add the drained gnocchi to the sauce with a little of the cooking water. Finish with a tiny pinch of sea salt and a little more grated Pecorino.

CARBONARA

Allow 80g of pasta per person

Serves 2

150g guanciale (cured pork cheek) or pancetta affumicata, cut into cubes

extra virgin olive oil, for frying (optional)

3 large, free-range egg yolks

75g Pecorino Romano, grated

small bunch of fresh parsley, roughly chopped (this is an upgrade on the original)

freshly milled black pepper, to taste

Parmigiano Reggiano, grated, to serve

Tip from the kitchen

Don't think for one minute this dish could be improved with cream. In the 1950s, in the post-war affluent era, and with the influence of French cooking (as this was seen as more sophisticated), traditional Italian recipes were changed. Carbonara is one of the classics; adding another ingredient will not make it better.

There was war 20 years ago when we first added this dish to the menu. We often felt like we were losing a battle introducing authentic dishes. For years, we had to fight with guests who asked where the cream and mushrooms were. I can't tell you how many TripAdvisor reviews we got complaining that our cooking wasn't Italian.

The *carbonai*, the charcoal burners originally from Naples, travelled to the north of Italy at the beginning of the nineteenth century. They would cook on open fires using what they could transport in their backpacks. Some pasta, a little cured pork, a few eggs and some aged Pecorino. This was street food, and a hundred years later it's now gourmet.

Making Carbonara for more than two at a time can be tricky, as you need a really big bowl to mix the egg mixture and I've always found it a bit tricky to get the egg to coat the pasta before it gets cold. Maybe that's where the saying 'two's company and three's a crowd' comes from.

Use spaghettini for this dish.

Bring a large pot of salted water to the boil. Add the spaghettini. The rest takes less time than the pasta needs to cook.

Set a frying pan on the heat and add the guanciale or pancetta. Lightly fry to render the fat. (You don't need to add oil to the pan unless it looks a little dry.)

In a large mixing bowl, add the egg yolks, the grated cheese, the parsley and several mills of black pepper. Beat with a fork.

When the pasta is cooked, drain it (leave it a little wet to help release the flavour from the pan) and add it to the guanciale/pancetta. Mix well.

Immediately add the cooked pasta and guanciale to the egg mixture. You must not transfer this back to the heat, otherwise you'll cook the egg and end up with scrambled pasta.

Serve immediately with a little grated Parmigiano.

CONTADINO

Allow 80g of pasta per person

Per person

25g dried porcini mushrooms

100g Cremini or Paris Brown mushrooms, washed and sliced

25g unsalted butter

Centotre fresh piccante sausage, steamed, cooled, skin removed and sliced

100ml double cream

50g Parmigiano Reggiano, grated, plus some to serve

sea salt flakes and freshly milled black pepper, to taste

handful of fresh rocket

We've sold more of this dish than any other. It has never left Contini George Street since we opened in April 2004. The word *contadino* means 'a man of the land'. To balance it out, order a Melograno salad.

We make this dish using fresh orecchiette pasta sourced from Puglia.

Soak the porcini in warm water for 30 minutes. Drain, reserving the broth and checking there is no grit in the remaining broth.

Boil the pasta in salted water.

Choose a large frying pan and fry the Cremini mushrooms in the butter until soft. Add the sausage, the porcini and half the mushroom liquid, and cook until it has reduced. Add the cream and simmer until it starts to thicken. Add the Parmigiano and check the seasoning.

Drain the pasta and add it to the sauce, with the rocket. The rocket will wilt in the heat.

Enjoy with more freshly grated Parmigiano.

Tip from the kitchen

There are believed to be over 350 different types of pasta. Knowing which shape to use with which sauce is part of an Italian's DNA. Trust the region and the restaurant.

AMATRICIANA

Allow 80g of pasta per person

Makes enough sugo for 2–3

1 small onion, cut in half lengthways and very finely sliced

1–2 tbsp extra virgin olive oil

1 dried chilli, crushed – it will give you a kick if you have a cold

150g guanciale, or pancetta affumicata, cut into small cubes

2 x tin (400g) best quality Italian plum tomatoes, liquidised

Pecorino Romano, grated, to serve

This is a dish from our region, Lazio. It's a pasta you'll see on every menu in Rome. It's made with cured pig's cheek, guanciale, but you can use pancetta or smoked bacon rashers as an alternative. Traditionally, this is eaten with bucatini pasta, which are long, thick tubes. Be prepared to get messy, as it's a skill to twirl without it splashing everywhere.

Choose a wide, shallow pan and gently fry the onion in oil until soft. The thin slices of onion are a key part of this dish. You don't want the onion chopped, so don't be tempted.

Next, add the chilli and guanciale, and cook until it colours and is slightly crispy. Don't let it get too brown, as you don't want it hard. Add the tomatoes and simmer for about 45 mins until the sugo is glossy.

Serve with your chosen pasta. This is best enjoyed with Pecorino, not Parmigiano; it's far more traditional, and the tartness of the Pecorino makes this taste so much better.

Tip from the kitchen

When in Rome . . . save up and book the Cavalieri Waldorf Astoria. It has probably the best swimming pool in the city, plus a very famous restaurant that has three Michelin stars (if that's your thing).

PUTTANESCA

Allow 80g of pasta per person

Per person

200g ripe Italian cherry tomatoes, washed and cut in half

2 anchovies, chopped

1 garlic clove, peeled and sliced

2 tbsp extra virgin olive oil

1 tbsp Taggiasche olives

sea salt flakes, to taste

This is the dish that makes me think of family in Italy – and family who are sadly no longer with us. Pauline, my first cousin, and Renzo, her husband, were our connection to Picinisco.

Aunty Lena, my father's elder sister, was a wild lady. Victor and I had been married for about seven years and had no babies yet . . . it was always a tough conversation, as you can imagine. Well, Aunty Lena, aged almost 90, lying literally on her death bed with her white nighty and bed jacket on, looking very regal, pulled back the sheets to our disbelief and faced Victor and I, and said, 'I'll show you how to do it.' Less than one year later, No. 1 son arrived. The shock must have worked.

Sadly, we no longer have Aunty Lena, Pauline or Renzo, but Renzo shared this dish with me in Picinisco when I was very much in love with Victor, but very far away from him, and very unsure of what our future would be.

Puttanesca, I should say, is the Italian for tart's pasta, not the sweet variety.

Serve with penne, for a change.

Add the tomatoes, anchovies, garlic and half the oil to a large frying pan and raise the heat. Add more oil as it cooks, to help emulsify the tomatoes as they start to separate and break down. Add the olives to heat them through, then season with salt. Add to the cooked penne.

Like many pasta dishes, this shouldn't be served with Parmigiano.

Tip from the kitchen

Wake up smiling for no reason. Your day will be better, I promise.

LINGUINE AI FRUTTI DI MARE

Allow 80g of pasta per person

Per person

2 tbsp extra virgin olive oil

1 small garlic clove, peeled and sliced

1 whole dried chilli, crushed

splash of dry white wine

120g cherry tomatoes, cut in half

small handful of clams, soaked in salted water to remove any grit

small handful of mussels, soaked in salted water to remove any grit

1 or 2 langoustine, cut down the spine to remove the digestive tract

small handful of fresh squid, washed and thinly sliced

generous handful of flat-leaf parsley, leaves only, finely chopped

sea salt flakes, to taste

When eaten with a glass of very crisp, dry Biancolella or Fiano, it's like you've won the lottery. Especially if you can eat this outside in the sunshine. I make this dish with linguine.

―――――

Choose a large frying pan and start by adding the oil, garlic and chilli, and gently heat. Add a little wine to the pan and cook enough to remove the alcohol. Next, add the tomatoes and cook for about 5 minutes until soft.

Add the shells, langoustine and the squid, and steam until the shells are open. The sauce is cooked. Add the parsley and season.

Add the cooked pasta and mix well.

Tip from the kitchen

Seafood pasta is never served with Parmigiano in Italy, or at Contini George Street.

Pesce

SCAMPI
con Burro al limone

Makes enough Burro al limone for about 20 large prawns

For the Burro al limone

200g unsalted butter, at room temperature

2 garlic cloves, crushed

1 dried chilli, crushed

juice of 1 unwaxed lemon

100g flat-leaf parsley, stalks removed, very finely chopped

sea salt flakes, to taste

I grew up with the sea as my neighbour and my father had a very good relationship with the local fishermen. The friendship deepened in the local pub, so there was never a shortage of shellfish in our house. Langoustines are called prawns in fishing villages around Scotland, so that's what I will be using for this recipe. There is something about butter and shellfish that has you licking your fingers.

Beat all the butter ingredients together.

To prepare the prawns, split them down their backs and remove the digestive sack and brain cavity. If they are alive, you will need to be attentive. Choose a large, sharp knife and very carefully hold the head between two fingers and insert the knife just below the eyes at the back of the head. Crack the shell all the way down the spine to split the prawn in two. Rinse under cold water, pat dry and set aside.

Generously fill the backs of each prawn with the flavoured butter and layer them on a large flat baking tray. Roast under a grill for 3–4 minutes or in a very hot oven (230°C/450°F/Gas 8) for about 4–5 minutes until the prawns are opaque.

Tip from the kitchen

The best langoustine should be alive when you get them. Enjoy if there is an 'R' in the month. The summer is the breeding season, due to warmer temperatures. The fishermen always stuck to that rule. In Britain, we use the word 'scampi' for prawns deep-fried in breadcrumbs. In Italy, scampi are langoustines.

CAPESANTE – SCALLOPS
con Gremolata

Allow 2–3 large scallops per person (coral and membrane removed)

unsalted butter, or extra virgin olive oil, depending on your preference

1 Amalfi lemon, cut into wedges

For the Gremolata
Makes enough for 8–9 scallops

zest of 2 unwaxed lemons, finely grated

1 garlic clove, finely grated

50g flat-leaf parsley, leaves only, very finely chopped

50g fresh fennel, fronds only, finely chopped

100g fresh breadcrumbs

sea salt flakes, to taste

glug of extra virgin olive oil

Scallops in any combination are always a bestseller.

Make the Gremolata first. Mix the lemon zest and the garlic in a bowl. Add the herbs and breadcrumbs. Season with salt and mix with enough oil to form a loose salsa.

Pat the scallops dry before you fry. Choose a non-stick pan. Heat with a little butter or extra virgin olive oil. Quickly add the scallops and cook for about 2 minutes until golden, then turn over to cook the other side. Drying the flesh helps them caramelise. Add more fat to the pan if required, and coat the scallops to keep them juicy.

The scallops will only take another minute or so, depending on their size. Overcooking them will make them tough.

When you are ready, drizzle the Gremolata over the scallops. If you have a grill, you can flash the dressed scallops very quickly to toast the breadcrumbs. Serve with a big wedge of Amalfi lemon.

Tip from the kitchen

Our chefs receive specific training to prepare whole scallops. Opening the shell and removing the membrane without damaging the mussel is a skill. Scallops do contain toxins and should be run under cold water for 10 minutes to purify them. When a restaurant offers to do the work for you, it's hard to resist.

CALAMARI FRITTI *Squid.*

Per person

300ml olive oil, to deep fry

100g plain white flour

2 tsp sea salt flakes

200g cleaned squid, thinly sliced, washed and dried well

Fritto misto, or mixed fried fish, is a standard dish for most coastal restaurants in the Mediterranean. Fresh fish from the local harbour dipped in seasoned flour and fried – never battered like the tradition we've adopted in the UK. Feel free to be adventurous; if you can get your hands on some fresh shrimp or sprats fried the same way, your calamari will be having a party.

Choose a heavy pot to fry the squid. This helps maintain a consistent temperature, if you don't have an electric deep-fat fryer.

Heat the oil to 188°C/370°F or until it is hot enough that if you add a piece of squid it will start to sizzle but not spit.

Add the flour and salt to a large bowl. Dip the squid in the flour and shake off any excess. Slowly add the squid to the oil and fry gently until golden; this should take about 3 or 4 minutes only. Remove and drain on some kitchen towel. Season with some more salt.

Tip from the kitchen

Fare la scarpetta translates to 'make the little school' – it's used when you ask permission at the table to take a piece of bread and wipe your plate clean. The cook will be flattered, and when you're with us, no need to ask.

MERLUZZO Cod
con Salsa verde

Serves 2

2 x 250g pieces of cod fillet with the skin on, washed and dried

drizzle of extra virgin olive oil

pinch of sea salt flakes, to taste

For the Salsa verde

50g flat-leaf parsley, leaves only

50g basil, leaves only

50g fresh mint, leaves only

1 garlic clove

2 salted anchovies

50g salted capers soaked for 2 mins and drained

pinch of sea salt flakes, to taste

1–2 tsp red wine vinegar, if you prefer a sharper finish

3–4 tbsp extra virgin olive oil

Salsa verde – green sauce – is a basic recipe that can sensationalise any meal. I love it the most with any roasted fish, especially cod.

If you have a frying pan that can go straight into the oven, that helps, but if not, have a baking sheet on hand.

Dry the fish on a piece of kitchen towel. Heat the pan and add a drizzle of oil. Place the cod, skin-side down, in the pan. It should make a lovely sizzle. Cook for 2 minutes to brown the skin, then turn over and cook for another minute. Remove from the pan and place on a baking sheet. Season with a little salt and another drizzle of oil and roast at 230°C/450°F/Gas 8 for 8 minutes until the fish is opaque all the way through.

Serve with the Salsa verde.

Salsa verde

Chop the herbs, garlic and anchovies on a wooden board. Transfer to a bowl and start to mix in the remaining ingredients. The capers should be left whole for extra texture. A pinch of salt helps, and add just enough vinegar to give a tang.

Tip from the kitchen

I used to make the Salsa verde in a pestle and mortar, but chopped and mixed is much nicer. Don't use a food processor – big mistake. I'm speaking from experience.

BRANZINO SEA BASS
con Spinaci e pomodori

Serves 2

150g–200g fillet of sea bass per person

For the Spinaci e pomodori

1 tbsp extra virgin olive oil

1 garlic clove, sliced

150g Pachino tomatoes

50g Taggiasche olives, pitted

2 handfuls of fresh spinach leaves

sea salt flakes, to taste

This is another classic dish from Contini George Street. Great cooking is about using the best, freshest ingredients and letting them do all the talking.

Cooking a whole fish takes a little confidence. It's amazing how a head and a tail can scare people off. If you've not 'tackled' it before, can I suggest you start with getting your lovely fishmonger to take the head off for you – then you just need to worry about the tail and the bone. Nothing to look back at you. Fillet of fish, especially if you're entertaining, can be a safer solution and just as tasty.

Dry the fish on a piece of kitchen towel. Heat the pan – it needs to be hot, so the skin doesn't stick – and add a drizzle of oil. Place the sea bass, skin-side down, in the pan. It should make a lovely sizzle. Gently move the pan to release the fish and help the skin crisp. The bass will start to curl at the edges, so that will help you see that the skin is getting crispy. Cook for 2–3 minutes until the fish easily releases from the pan. If it sticks, that usually means it isn't ready to turn. Lower the heat slightly and cook until opaque.

For the sauce, drizzle some oil into a medium-sized frying pan and add the garlic and tomatoes. Increase the heat to high to help split the skins of the tomatoes to release their juices. Lower the heat and add the olives and the spinach. Steam for about 2 or 3 minutes until the leaves have wilted slightly. Season with salt and serve with the sea bass.

Tip from the kitchen

Fish are all different thicknesses depending on the age and type. As long as the flesh is opaque it's ready to eat.

SGOMBRO Mackerel (SCOTLAND) Sardines

Serves 2

4 mackerel fillets, or
6 sardine fillets

50g pine kernels, toasted lightly and allowed to cool

50g sultanas

zest of 1 lemon

1 tbsp of extra virgin olive oil

large handful of fresh parsley, leaves only, chopped

100g fresh breadcrumbs

sea salt flakes and freshly milled black pepper, to taste

Mackerel is easy to get all year in Scotland. Sardines, which are an abundant Sicilian catch, seasonally swim up to Cornish waters from July onwards. Both fish have a rich flavour and oily quality. Either will work for this recipe.

Wash and dry the fish and lay it skin-side down on a flat roasting tray.

Mix the remaining ingredients together with enough oil to combine without making them too oily, if that makes sense. Generously scatter over the fillets.

Bake at 180°C/350°F/Gas 4 for 12–15 minutes until the fish is cooked and the crumb is crisp. Enjoy with a light green salad.

Tip from the kitchen

Gently rub your fingers against the grain of the flesh of the fillets of any fish. If there are any fine bones this is when you'll be able to catch them and tweeze them out.

CAMPANIA

Campania is our favourite food region.

Victor's father, Nonno Carlo, was born just outside Naples in the little Roman town of Pozzuoli. It lies about 20 miles up the coast and houses the Flavian Amphitheatre, the third largest Roman theatre in the world. Designed by the same architect who built the Colosseum, you can see that size said it all in AD 70. If you know Rome, then visit Naples. It leaves you struck by just how many treasures Italy has but struggles to know what to do with. In Rome, you feel like everything is cherished and preserved. In Naples, it's a whole other story.

Mount Vesuvius dominates Naples. It is beautiful and bewitching in equal measure. One day it will speak as it did back in AD 79.

The expression '*vedi Napoli e poi muori*' ('see Naples and die') has many meanings. With the noise, the bustle and the commotion, it can feel like you are taking your life in your hands just crossing the street. We love Naples for the place, the people and, of course, the pizza. When we think of Naples, it's hard to think about anything else.

The original home of pizza is believed to be Pizzeria Brandi. Opened by Pietro 'il Pizzaiulo' in 1780 and then passed to the Brandi family, it has been run by them ever since. In 1889, they prepared pizza for Queen Margherita at a ball in Capodimonte, a magnificent palazzo overlooking the city. Pizza Margherita was born. Arianna, daughter No. 2, chose Margherita as her confirmation name. I wonder why . . .

Leaving the tablecloths at Brandi, the best place for pizza has to be the rustic, rough-and-ready Da Michele. You can queue for hours. The choice: Margherita (with cheese) or Marinara (without). Coke, Peroni or water. The master 'pizzaiolo' (now without a 'u') ceremoniously drizzles the final touch of oil before the dough heads into the wood-fired oven. Paying the bill at the cassa, the owner has a cigarette dangling from his mouth with a commanding 'Vietato Fumare' sign directly above his head. The things you'll only see in Naples.

Naples is usually the departure point for either a drive down to Amalfi or to board the *traghetto* from the port of Mergellina to the island of Ischia. Queuing to board, then sitting on the top deck looking back towards the city, we know we're on holiday. Growing up on the coast in Scotland, between two harbours, has instilled for all the family a great love of and huge respect for the sea. These trips on the open-top ferries, with the sun smiling down on you, either start your holiday or finish it in comfort, warmth and style.

Great food is always just a mouthful away on Ischia. Da Raffaele is our favourite trattoria. Being restaurateurs, we always tend to find a restaurant that's good and stick to it for the whole holiday.

I recall one visit years ago. Victor ordered his favourite, Zuppe di Cozze. If you know Victor, you know Victor. My bias aside, he genuinely connects with people. I struggle to be so open and relaxed with strangers, but Victor is a natural. My darling husband ordered 'un bel piatto di zuppe di cozze' from Raffaele. 'Mussels are light! Ahha! For you and me, that's three normal portions.'

After a laugh and a joke, a large, beautiful hand-painted bowl arrived, steaming with open shells of loveliness and finished with shards of bruschetta dotted around the cozze. He got stuck in. Not a word was spoken. Then all hell broke out. 'Io sono un grand giornalista d' America' was heard being shouted from the other end of the room and this very glamorous lady stormed out. It turned out she'd ordered the cozze but without the 'bel piatto supplemento'. The owner was in a tizzy; he was close to tears. Victor was paying for three portions of mussels – it wasn't as if he was getting a free meal – but this lady was having none of it. The lesson for us: never ask for anything special in a restaurant, unless you're willing to pay the consequences.

COZZE Mussels

Serves 2–3 (or Victor)

1 x (500g) tin Italian plum tomatoes

extra virgin olive oil

1 or 2 garlic cloves, sliced

2–3 dried or fresh chillies, to your taste, crushed

splash of white wine

1kg spanking fresh mussels, soaked in several changes of ice-cold water and cleaned

sea salt flakes, to taste

large handful of fresh flat-leaf parsley (leaves only), chopped

This is one of the lowest calorie dishes – not that we count, but when Victor's pretending to be on a diet, this is what he orders.

Make the tomato base first. Choose a large, heavy-bottomed casserole. I've got a brilliant wide, deep pot with a lid that I love using for this, as it holds way more than 'un bel piatto' and it is shallow enough that the mussels are well spaced out and can open easily. Take each plum tomato and roughly chop it into 6–8 pieces. I like this texture, rather than a puree.

Add enough oil to lightly coat the bottom of the pot. Add the garlic and chilli. We love a real kick, so add lots. Allow the garlic and chilli to sizzle but not brown. Add a few glugs of wine and cook to burn off the alcohol. The wine adds a lovely depth to the sauce and makes the final dish just that little bit more elegant.

Next, add the tomatoes. Remember to rinse the tins with a little cold water and add to the pot. Stir and simmer for about 20 minutes until the tomatoes look glossy and silky. You don't want them to be overcooked. Add more extra virgin olive oil if you feel it's looking too dry. Good oil only adds to the flavour; it's hard to add too much.

Strain the mussels and add them to the hot sauce. Cover with a lid and steam until all the shells are open. I usually shake the pot once or twice throughout the cooking to get the flavour of the tomatoes into the mussels and to move the shells around to help them open. This will take about 4 or 5 minutes only. Season with a little salt and the chopped parsley.

Enjoy with chunks of old bread lightly fried in a little oil and then sprinkled with salt. They provide the perfect sponge to soak up all the lovely juices.

Tip from the kitchen

The sign of a good fish restaurant is clean mussels. When you are preparing them, scrape off any barnacles and remove the beard. Leave the mussels in a large bowl covered with cold water. Any mussels that float need to be binned; any mussels that don't open once you've cooked them mustn't be eaten. Don't be tempted to keep either.

PESCE AL FORNO

Serves 3–4

1½–2kg whole fish, gutted, scales removed, washed and dried

handful of fresh fennel fronds, left whole

handful of fresh parsley

2 bulbs of fennel, trimmed and finely sliced

2 unwaxed lemons, finely sliced

2 tbsp extra virgin olive oil

1 tsp sea salt flakes

It's far more common in Italy to order a whole fish in a restaurant that you share with your guests. The very talented waiter, after helping you choose the fish in advance, usually the most expensive available at the time, will bring the beauty, once cooked, back to the table. He will usually debone and fillet it for you. I'm a control freak and like to do it myself.

Choose a flat baking tray that the fish will be able to lie in and drizzle with extra virgin olive oil. You don't want it too deep, as you want the heat of the oven to bake the fish all around, but it needs to be deep enough to hold the juices that will escape as the fish bakes.

Place the herbs inside the fish to add a little extra fragrance. Score a few lines on the flesh of the fish, as this helps it cook, then place the fish onto the tray.

Mix the fennel slices, lemon slices, oil and salt together and then spoon around the fish. I like cooking it this way, as the juices mix together.

Bake at 200°C/400°F/Gas 6 for 20 minutes per kilo until the white flesh releases easily from the bone and is cooked all the way through. Remove the fish onto a large board. Serve with the fennel and lemon as a dressing.

Some restaurants will serve whole baked fish deboned and dressed with a mixture of raw red onion, olives, cooked salad potatoes and tomatoes that have been marinated in olive oil and salt with lots of fresh parsley. If you see alla Catalana on a menu, order – it won't disappoint.

Tip from the kitchen

Be very careful when serving whole fish, as the bones can be very fine and can get lost. Start by removing the fennel and lemon and set aside. Next, remove the head and tail. Take your knife down the spine of the fish all the way to the tail. Remove this and the fins. Scrape off the skin, then release the top fillet from the spine and place it on a serving plate. This should now reveal the spine; remove it and the bottom fillet will be revealed.

GRANCHIO

Serves 2–3

1 fennel bulb, green stalks and core removed, finely chopped

1 cucumber, peeled and seeds removed, chopped

1 spring onion, very finely chopped

50g fresh parsley, leaves only, very finely chopped

25g fresh dill, fronds only, very finely chopped

25g fresh chives, very finely chopped

25g baby salted capers, rinsed

zest and juice of 1 unwaxed lemon

1 large cooked crab (ask your lovely fishmonger to clean the meat from the shell and set it aside for you)

100g watermelon chunks, no seeds

sea salt flakes and freshly milled black pepper, to taste

2 tbsp light extra virgin olive oil

This crab salad is so refreshing and incredibly light. The small crispy bites of the vegetables are a lovely contrast. It probably belongs up in Liguria, sitting very happily in Portofino.

I'm not a gadget girl. I resist buying kitchen equipment, as often you use it once and it is left to gather dust. A good knife, however, is an essential. For this salad, you want the fennel to be trimmed and chopped as finely as the smallest Lego blocks. Be patient with your sharp knife and chopping board. Once chopped, place in a large bowl.

Chop the cucumber and set it aside in a separate bowl with some kitchen towel to help it dry.

Chop the spring onion, then the herbs: the finer the leaves, the better. Add these to the bowl, along with the capers and the cucumber. Grate the zest from the lemon and add to the bowl. Add the crab and watermelon, season and finish with the oil and lemon juice. Mix well.

Refrigerate for half an hour or so and enjoy chilled with lovely hot garlicky Bruschetta (p. 45).

Tip from the kitchen

Andrea Bocelli's version of 'Love In Portofino' goes very well with this dish.

PESCE AL TAGLIO HALIBUT

Per person

unsalted butter

200g fillet of halibut, skin removed

4 tbsp double cream

25g Parmigiano Reggiano, grated

squeeze of lemon juice

sea salt flakes, to taste

½ fresh black truffle (if available), grated to serve

Victor loves a hobby. Unfortunately, the hobbies get neglected when life, and more typically work, takes over. Victor now has a new hobby that he says will also be work, so he thinks he's won the argument.

Daddy and daughter No. 2 have a puppy. He wanted a Lagotto Romagnolo, the only breed of dog trained to hunt truffles, but in the end he got a cocker spaniel. Rocco is better than any Lagotto, in my eyes. Victor is determined they'll find truffles in Scotland. We'll keep you posted.

Choose a flat ceramic baking dish, rub with a little butter and place the halibut on the dish. Pour the cream over the fish. Add the Parmigiano and lemon juice, and season with salt. Bake for 10–12 minutes at 230°C/450°F/Gas 8 until the cheese is golden. Serve with freshly grated black truffle, if available.

Tip from the kitchen

Fresh truffles are a special ingredient, even I have to admit. What puts me off is the artificial taste of truffle oil so often used as a fake and cheap substitute. Never buy this. White is a luxury most can't afford. Black is a subtle delight worth enjoying.

ARAGOSTA

Allow 80g linguine per person

Serves 2-3

1.5kg lobster

1 unwaxed lemon, skin and pith removed and segments taken from the fruit

50g flat-leaf parsley, leaves only

50g fresh dill, fronds only

1 fresh red chilli, seeds removed and very finely chopped

pinch of sea salt flakes

4 tbsp extra virgin olive oil (last season's oil from Lazio or Liguria is perfect for this, as you don't want a new season oil to overpower the lobster)

Lobster can sometimes feel too light, as it's so expensive. Adding a carbohydrate is necessary to make you feel as if you've not broken the bank and that your tummy is satisfied. This lobster is a pasta dressing – because, what's the saying . . . Life is too short not to eat lobster linguine.

Place the lobster claws in a pot of cold water. Bring to the boil and simmer for 5 minutes. Remove from the heat. Leave in the water until cool enough to handle. Crack the claws in the middle with a mallet. Remove the shell to reveal the flesh. It doesn't matter if the flesh is broken, as you want to flake it into small pieces anyway.

Place the lobster in a pot of cold, slightly salted water. Bring the water to the boil, simmer for 2 minutes and then turn off the heat. Allow the water to cool long enough so that you can handle the lobster.

Remove the head from the tail. This just needs some courage and a little strength. Make sure there is a sink below you, as it can be messy. Cut the tail in half and remove the digestive tract. Remove the flesh from the shell and cut each half into 3 or 5 pieces.

Place all the lobster meat into a large bowl. Add the lemon segments, parsley, dill, chilli and salt, and dress with the oil. Mix thoroughly. Leave at room temperature.

Boil the linguine and, when al dente, drain and toss in the lobster dressing. Add a little of the reserved cooking water and some extra olive oil to finish the dish and make the sauce.

Tip from the kitchen

Never buy a lobster that weighs less than 1lb. These are babies that should be thrown back into the sea.

Carne

EMILIA-ROMAGNA

Emilia-Romagna is the home of Parmigiano Reggiano, Prosciutto di Parma, mortadella, zampone, culatello and Aceto Balsamico di Modena. All hefty, Olympic record foods. Many you will find in the best restaurants around the world, and all of them are in our fridge at home and at Contini George Street.

The city that gets the praise as the stock pot for these ingredients is Bologna. There are certain cities that leave their mark; Bologna leaves its taste.

The unique arcades that line the city, keeping you cool in the shade, create a pleasant walking environment that many other Italian cities don't share in the blazing height of the summer. If only Edinburgh had copied Bologna, walking in the city would be far more pleasant when you're being torn by a gale.

Formerly the home of the Communist Party, while Italy has traditionally been socialist, Bologna has a slightly anarchic, medieval uncertainty about it. Its real jewels are its food markets; the most famous, off the Piazza Maggiore, is the Mercato di

Mezzo. Fruit and vegetables spill out on to the narrow street, with everything you could wish to eat. Heavenly delis dedicated to one or two ingredients allow you to indulge in the delights freshly cut from their counters.

Modena, despite its status as the high altar of the vinegars of the world, is pretty and petite. Italy is so spoiled with its super cities that little gems like Modena and even Parma can feel left behind. Still, with Massimo Bottura's Osteria Francescana – and its reputation as the number one restaurant in the world – it might not be overlooked. Thanks to the town's ingredients and this famous chef, Modena is certainly now on the map.

RAGÙ

Serves 6

1–2 tbsp extra virgin olive oil

2 medium onions, finely chopped

2 medium carrots, finely chopped

1kg finely ground best steak mince

sea salt flakes and freshly milled black pepper, to taste

3 tbsp of milk

splash of white wine (white wine like a Trebbiano is traditional, never red)

500–750ml passata, or blended plum tomatoes (depending on how saucy you like it)

My family doesn't come from Bologna but we have a tradition of cooking ragù, a variation on the same theme of Bolognese. This is my version. Enjoy with a flat egg (preferably fresh) pasta.

Choose a heavy-based casserole pot and gently fry the onions in the oil until soft but not brown. Add the carrots and gently coat in the oil. Cook until golden but not browned. Add the mince, and cook until brown and the meat has broken down with no lumps. Be patient, this takes a little time and a lot of stirring. Season generously with salt and freshly milled black pepper. Add the milk and cook until it has evaporated – this tenderises the meat. Add the wine and cook until evaporated. Then add the passata. Rinse the jar with half the volume of water and add to the pot.

Cover with a lid and bake in the oven for 1 hour 45 minutes to 2 hours at 220°C/425°F/Gas 7 until the meat is tender and the sauce has started to thicken. You'll see that the edges of the pot show the sauce has concentrated. Don't worry if this looks very brown, or even burned; you need time to bring out the flavour.

Tip from the kitchen

If you eat Bolognese in Bologna, some restaurants use tomatoes while others don't. It will always be served with a flat egg pasta – tagliatelle or, as the Americans call it, fettuccine. Fettuccine is just a slightly thicker version of tagliatelle. One is from Bologna, the other is from Rome. One day I'm going to take a degree in pasta. Some restaurants will add offal (heart and lungs) into the recipe, not uncommon additions. It's not awful . . . (sorry – bad joke).

OSSOBUCO
con Gremolata di Selina e Risotto alla Milanese

Serves 4

extra virgin olive oil, for frying

1 onion, peeled and very finely chopped

1–2 sticks of celery, very finely chopped (save the tops of the celery for the end)

1 carrot, peeled and very finely chopped

1–2 pieces of fresh fennel, trimmed and very finely chopped (save the fennel fronds until the end)

sea salt flakes and freshly milled black pepper, to taste

4 shins of veal

plain flour, for coating the veal

100ml white wine, such as a Pinot bianco

4 sprigs of fresh thyme

1 sprig of fresh rosemary

Italy is made up of 20 very different regions and the cooking is unique to each. Local recipes have transported incredibly well across the world. Ossobuco is a classic dish from Lombardy made from shin of veal slowly braised and served with a saffron risotto and finished with gremolata. Lake Garda is in Lombardy and I always think this dish looks like a little island surrounded by a lake of luscious, golden glossy rice.

First prepare the soffritto. In a wide-based casserole pot or a frying pan, heat the oil. It's really important that all the vegetables are chopped as finely as possible. Add the onion and cook for a few minutes, then add the celery, carrot and fennel and sweat until tender. Season.

In a separate large frying pan, heat some oil. Dip the veal in flour and add to the hot oil. Cook both sides until golden. Remove from the heat. Transfer the veal into a deep ovenproof dish and add the soffritto.

Return the frying pan used for the veal to the heat and pour in the wine. Keep stirring the pan to release all the flour. This will help to thicken the juices of the ossobuco. Reduce the wine by half, then pour it through a sieve over the veal. This is to remove any lumps of flour.

Put the pan back on the heat and add enough water to create a sauce, but not too much, as this can make the meat stew rather than gently roast. Heat until the water is boiling, then pour over the veal, again passing through a sieve first.

Season and add the herbs, cover with tin foil and place in an oven (190°C/375°F/Gas 5) for 2–2½ hours.

During the cooking time, check the meat and turn it. If it's still tough and looking dry, add some more water. The juices should be creamy and glossy. The meat has to be falling off the bone when it's ready. This takes time – give it more, if it needs it.

At the very end, add the finely chopped celery leaves and the fennel fronds. Next, prepare the gremolata and risotto.

Gremolata di Selina

Gremolata di Selina

zest of 1 unwaxed orange

zest of 2 unwaxed lemons

1 garlic clove

pinch of sea salt flakes

100g fresh parsley, leaves only, very finely chopped

4 tbsp extra virgin olive oil

This recipe has a special extra ingredient compared to our normal gremolata and that's thanks to my sister-in-law, Selina. The orange makes this sparkle.

———

Finely zest the orange and lemon rind, and set aside. Using a pestle and mortar, grind the garlic with a pinch of salt until you have a smooth paste. Add the parsley and a little extra virgin olive oil to loosen. Add the zest. The gremolata should be piccante and tangy.

You only need a teaspoon for each piece of veal, but the gremolata lifts the flavour and helps cut the fatness and richness of the meat.

Risotto alla Milanese

Risotto alla Milanese

Serves 4

100g unsalted butter

1 shallot, very finely grated (I never chop the onion, as inevitably you end up with a piece in your mouth; grated is much better)

200g Vialone Nano risotto rice

splash of white wine, Pinot grigio style

2 tsp saffron, soaked in a little stock

1 litre (approx.) chicken stock

200g Parmigiano Reggiano, freshly grated

Ossobuco is best served with Risotto alla Milanese. Traditionally, this dish is made with a rich mutton stock, but here I use its lighter cousin, chicken stock.

———

Melt a quarter of the butter and add the shallot. Cook very slowly until it's soft. Add the rice and toast. Be careful not to burn the rice. If you do, it won't absorb the liquid and won't cook. Next, add the wine and cook until it has evaporated.

Add the saffron and the stock, a ladle at a time, until it's absorbed. Keep stirring the risotto. Slowly add enough stock, cooking the liquid off until the rice is al dente. Add the remaining butter, stir, then leave covered, off the heat, for 5 minutes.

Finally, add the Parmigiano, then check the seasoning, as the Parmigiano can be salty.

Tip from the kitchen

When making risotto, it's a bit like making porridge. Tradition says you must only stir clockwise. Sinister comes from the Latin word *sinistra*, meaning evil, and in Italian it means 'left'. Stir as you wish, as long as you do it lots. That's the magic.

FEGATO ALLA VENEZIANA

Serves 2

1 large white onion, cut in half and very finely sliced (Italian white onions tend to be sweeter, so choose wisely)

2 dried chillies, crushed

extra virgin olive oil, for frying

250g calves' liver, cut into thin slices

2 tbsp white wine vinegar, or balsamic vinegar (it is richer but not traditional)

sea salt flakes and freshly milled black pepper, to taste

For the Crema di Patate

500g fluffy potatoes, (such as Maris Piper) peeled and diced

20ml light extra virgin olive oil

sea salt flakes, to taste

¼ nutmeg, freshly grated

2 tbsp double cream

I can think of few dishes to cook as quickly as Fegato alla Veneziana. If you overcook the liver, you'll go from melt in the mouth to tough love – there is nothing worse. This has to be veal or calves' liver. No other will do.

Fry the onion and chillies in the oil until soft. Remove and raise the heat of the pan. Add the liver and cook for 1 minute until it has changed colour. Return the onion and chillies to the pan and add the vinegar. Season.

Serve immediately with soft or grilled polenta, preferably the white variety, or it's delicious with Crema di Patate.

Crema di Patate

Boil the potatoes in unsalted water until very soft. Mash and add the oil, then season. Finish with the grated nutmeg and whip in the cream with a fork at the very end until fluffy.

Tip from the kitchen

Balsamic vinegar from Emilia-Romagna has to be a minimum of five years old before it can be called Aceto Balsamico di Modena. The real deal is sadly often faked by concocting red wine vinegar with added caramel to give the sweetness that the traditional 25-year authentic ingredient is characteristically known for. What makes me most frustrated is that this imposter appears all over the world. It seems to be the standard bearer for all dressings. Resist. Try a brilliant extra virgin olive oil and a squeeze of fresh lemon. Our family loves red wine vinegar as a salad dressing, too. Refreshingly alternative.

CONIGLIO ALL'ISCHITANA

Serves 4

2 tbsp extra virgin olive oil

2 garlic cloves, left whole

1 rabbit (or chicken, if you don't like to eat bunnies), cut into pieces

sea salt flakes and freshly milled black pepper, to taste

small glass of white wine

500g cherry tomatoes, washed and cut in half

100g Taggiasche olives

1 sprig of rosemary

1 sprig of thyme

few sprigs of tarragon

Rabbit is very much a country dish and famed on the island of Ischia.

Choose a heavy-bottomed casserole pot with a lid. Heat the oil and gently cook the garlic, not letting the cloves burn. Add the rabbit and brown. Season well and then add the wine to deglaze the pan.

Next add the tomatoes, olives and the herbs. Add 1–2 small cups of boiling water to the juices and release the sticky bits from the bottom of the pot. Cover and roast in the oven at 220°C/425°F/Gas 7 for 1–1½ hours until tender.

Tip from the kitchen

If you dine in a restaurant that specialises in rabbit, your first course is often pasta made with the sugo from the stew. The star of the afternoon, the second course, is the rabbit. This is usually served with the most gorgeous roast olive oil potatoes and a huge big bowl of salad for sharing. The head of the family always gets the head of the rabbit. I'm happy to be very far down the line at number 8. We've many happy memories of dining in the mountains and losing an afternoon rabbiting on.

MILANESE
con Salsa di noci

Per person

1 veal T-bone, French trimmed, or chicken breast

25g plain flour

1 free-range egg, beaten

100g fresh breadcrumbs (you can mix in 10g of grated Parmigiano Reggiano for a change, if you like)

25g unsalted butter, plus 10g extra to finish

1 tbsp extra virgin olive oil

sea salt flakes, to taste

1 Amalfi lemon, cut into wedges, to serve

For the Salsa di noci

100g walnuts

1 slice white bread, edges removed and roughly chopped

100ml milk

1 small garlic clove

50g Parmigiano Reggiano

zest of 1 unwaxed lemon

extra virgin olive oil

sea salt flakes and freshly milled black pepper, to taste

You can make this classic with veal, pork or chicken, to your budget or taste desires. Our favourite is a veal T-bone, French trimmed – the French trim cuts the fat off and releases part of the cutlet from the bone. This makes it easier to be beaten flat until it's thin. It's wildly expensive. A chicken breast, flattened by cutting the sinew and butterflying, is the favourite in the restaurant.

At home I like serving this with a rocket and Parmigiano salad, dressed with lemon and Sofia's Olive Oil. Simple, tasty and comforting. In the restaurant the team are far more adventurous, serving this with Gremolata (p. 102) and the most beautiful almond puree. Simply blend equal parts of cooled, lightly roasted almonds with boiling water and a little salt. No. 2 daughter loves a slightly more luscious version, Salsa di noci. The recipe for this is below.

Dip the meat in the flour, then the egg and then coat in the breadcrumbs.

Heat the butter and oil until they start to bubble. For the chicken, cook for about 3–4 minutes until golden, then turn and cook the other side. Transfer onto an ovenproof dish and add a little of the extra butter on top of each piece of chicken. Bake in an oven at 180°C/350°F/Gas 4 for 10–15 minutes until the butter has melted and the chicken is cooked all the way through.

For the veal, it will take at least 20 minutes to cook. Brown in the pan and then finish in the oven with a little extra butter. Sometimes restaurants serve this pink, but I like it cooked all the way through. Patience is a 'veal' virtue.

Check the seasoning and serve with a big wedge of fresh Amalfi lemon.

Salsa di noci

Roast the walnuts and allow to cool. Soak the bread in the milk. Blend the garlic and walnuts in a processor until powdered and add the soaked bread. Fold in the Parmigiano, lemon zest and enough oil to form a dressing.

Tip from the kitchen

The first time Victor and I went to Italy, we stayed in Sant'Agata, a beautiful village above Sorrento. In one restaurant I asked for Risotto alla Milanese. The waiter said, 'You're not in Milan, so why order this dish?' They shouldn't have had it on the menu. But it's a lesson that I learned over 30 years ago, and it's stuck with me. Milanese this way, when you're frying, can be eaten anywhere.

SALSICCIA

Serves 4

1 whole onion, finely chopped

1 tbsp extra virgin olive oil

250ml Italian plum tomatoes, cut into chunks

8 fresh Italian sausages

2 sprigs of fresh rosemary

250g Castelluccio lentils, rinsed

500ml hot vegetable stock or hot water

sea salt flakes and freshly milled black pepper, to taste

Really good Italian sausages slowly cooked in a tomato sugo, served with soft polenta... I'm in my happy place. It's sausages and mash for Italians.

We get our 100 per cent pork sausages made for us with our secret recipe of chilli flakes, fennel seeds, coriander seeds and black peppercorns. All grow wild in the Lazio mountains, where we come from.

Choose a heavy-bottomed casserole pot and gently cook the onion in the oil until golden. Add the tomatoes and when it's hot add the sausages and the rosemary. Next add the lentils, then enough of the stock to cover the ingredients. Season and simmer for 45 minutes until the sausages are cooked and the lentils are tender.

Remove the rosemary stalk and any small leaves, as they can be bitter. Serve with soft polenta (see p. 40) and some Mostarda di frutta.

Tip from the kitchen

Mostarda di frutta is another treasure from Modena. It's always on our Christmas table, as the colours of the beautiful candied mustard fruits are everything about the festive season – bright, intense, luxurious and totally delicious. Mostarda di frutta is not just for Christmas, it's great with some grilled meats, these sausages or a heavenly Bollito misto (p. 136).

BOLLITO MISTO
con Salsa Inglese

Serves 4

700ml hot chicken stock

400ml passata

4 chicken breasts, skin and wing on to get extra flavour

4 fresh Italian sausages, 125g each

20cm of spicy cured Italian sausage, cut into 4 pieces

600g spale bone or brisket, cut into two pieces to help it cook more evenly. On an odd, very special occasion I have used a piece of fillet steak – totally melt in the mouth

4 shallots, peeled and left whole

2 large carrots, peeled and cut in half

2 sticks celery, cleaned and cut in half

1 fennel bulb, trimmed and cut into quarters

handful of thyme, rosemary and parsley, tied with string

For the Salsa Inglese

600g milk

1 onion, studded with cloves

1 garlic clove

1 star anise

1 bay leaf

100g white bread, crusts removed and cut into small pieces

1 nutmeg, freshly grated

4 tbsp double cream

sea salt flakes and freshly milled black pepper, to taste

Verona is the home of the best bollito. Many restaurants will serve the array of meats from a trolley that's brought to your table and carve them in front of you. It's an old-fashioned spectacle. The beauty of this dish is you get a bit of everything. Don't plan this for a quick lunch; it is for relaxing and enjoying.

This dish should always be served with a variety of sauces. The classics include Salsa verde (p. 105) and Salsa rossa. If you want to add a Scots Italian feel, I love this with bread sauce – let's call it Salsa Inglese!

This is best cooked in a deep tray in the oven.

Place the tray or pot on the heat. Add the stock and the passata, and bring to a simmer. Very carefully place the meat and the vegetables into the hot liquid. Add the herbs. Cover with a lid, or some tin foil, if you are using a tray, and transfer to the oven and simmer very gently for about 1–1½ hours until all the meat is tender. Serve with Salsa Inglese.

Salsa Inglese

Bread sauce has medieval origins. It's seen as a very British sauce served at Christmas with turkey or goose, but many versions of it have accompanied bollito through the ages in Italy. This is my classic go-to recipe for both traditions. The cloves, star anise and nutmeg can so easily sit in either continent and in any century.

Simmer the milk with the onion, garlic, star anise and bay leaf, then remove from the heat. Leave to allow the flavours to release for about 20 minutes. Drain the milk over the bread and return to the heat. Simmer for about 5 minutes until the bread has started to break down. Remove from the heat and very lightly puree. Season with freshly grated nutmeg. Add the cream and bring back to a simmer. Check seasoning and serve warm.

Tip from the kitchen

Choosing the right wine does make a difference. Something as fabulous as a bollito needs a fabulous wine to accompany it. Victor would recommend a delicious Dolcetto or Barbera. If the company is as good as the food and the wine, you're in for a very happy evening.

POLLO

Serves 4

1.5kg free-range or organic chicken

zest of 2 unwaxed lemons

juice of 1 lemon

4 garlic cloves, whole, skin removed

extra virgin olive oil, to drizzle

500g waxy new potatoes, washed and cut in half

sea salt flakes and freshly milled black pepper, to taste

handful of parsley, leaves only

2 fresh red chillies, deseeded and very finely chopped

The old joke when Nonna G used to call on a Sunday night was that she'd start by saying, 'How was the roast chicken?' I used to be frightened to say we'd had anything different, as she might have a heart attack. Roast chicken (now two roast chickens, as the family is so big) is a Sunday staple. This recipe is my simplest fail-safe fast version.

Wash and dry the chicken, trimming any excess fat from the neck or the tail of the bird. Remove the back bone and cut the chicken into 6 pieces, 3 each side: leg and thigh and breast cut in half.

Mix the lemon zest, the juice of 1 lemon and the garlic, and marinate the chicken for about 30 minutes.

Drizzle a little extra virgin olive oil on the bottom of a roasting tray and place the chicken pieces and potatoes in the dish.

Season generously with salt and pepper. Drizzle some more extra virgin olive oil on top.

Preheat the oven to 220°C/425°F/Gas 7. Roast for 30 minutes until the skin starts to crisp.

Mix the parsley, chilli, a tablespoon of extra virgin olive oil and some salt, and brush over the chicken. Return to the oven at 180°C/350°F/Gas 4 and cook for another 45 mins or so, until crispy, golden and tender.

By adding the chilli and parsley at this stage, it stops the parsley burning.

Tip from the kitchen

Jersey Royal or Charlotte potatoes are best. Leave their skins on to keep them crispy.

PORCHETTA
con Salsa di salvia

Serves 8–10

whole loin of free-range pork, boned, scored and skin on

sea salt flakes and freshly milled black pepper, to taste

4 fennel bulbs, cut into quarters

250ml white wine

extra virgin olive oil

For the Salsa di salvia

6 large garlic cloves, peeled

100g fresh sage, leaves only

100g fennel fronds, no stalks, roughly chopped

6–8 tbsp extra virgin olive oil

3 tsp whole peppercorns

3 tsp sea salt flakes

6 tsp fennel seeds

sea salt flakes and freshly milled black pepper, to taste

There are some foods you taste when you're on holiday or living abroad that connect you to that place. Kebabs say Istanbul to me. Green oranges say Cairo. Fresh lime soda says Chennai. A salt beef sandwich says New York. These are often simple and cheap impressions on the palate but they leave a lifelong love bite on the soul.

In the beautiful town of Treviso in Veneto, there was (I hope it's still there) a traditional porchetta stall tucked under the town's bell tower. The taste of that porchetta panino still makes me hungry for more. Normally the whole pig, or a suckling pig, is used for a porchetta. Even I'm challenged to find and cook a whole pig, so this recipe is for the pork loin.

I've added a delicious Salsa di salvia to use as the stuffing.

Begin with the Salsa di salvia. Using a pestle and mortar, cream the garlic. Add the sage leaves and fennel fronds and a little oil until you have formed a paste. Add the peppercorns and crunch a little, but not too much – you want a little texture. Finally, fold in the salt and the fennel seeds. The mixture should be quite wet, so add more oil if required, as you want to rub this all over the pork, though it should feel almost like a stuffing. Check the seasoning.

You'll need a large clean working surface to prepare the porchetta.

Lay the pork loin skin-side down. Season with a little salt and freshly milled black pepper, then massage the Salsa di salvia all over the inside of the meat. Roll the loin lengthways and, using butcher's string, tie and knot it all the way down so it's nice and tight. This takes a little practice, but it's easy once you get started.

Place the loin in the fridge for at least 4 hours, or overnight, for the flavours to penetrate into the meat.

Remove from the fridge at least 30 minutes before you plan to cook.

Choose a large baking tray. Place the quarters of the fennel bulbs in the tray and the loin skin-side up on top. Mine always has to sit diagonally.

In order to get really good crispy crackling, the skin of the loin needs to be dry to start with. Leaving the loin out helps to air dry the skin naturally. A few sheets of kitchen roll to rub it down will help.

When you're ready to cook, generously rub the loin with olive oil and sprinkle liberally with salt.

To calculate how long this will need in the oven, check the total weight and allow 30 minutes per kilo. I'd suggest you place it in a hot oven (220°C/425°F/Gas 7) for 30 minutes until the skin is golden and starting to crackle. Add the white wine to the dish, but not over the crackling, as this will make it soggy. Cook for another hour. I don't baste the porchetta until the crackling is crisp and brittle. Cover loosely with tin foil, as you don't want the crackling to burn, and return to the oven for the remaining time, or until the meat runs clear when you pierce it with a sharp knife.

I gently peel or crack the crackling off the loin when I take it out of the oven. It tends to split nicely between the butcher's string. Leave this on a plate uncovered.

Separately cover the loin with fresh tin foil and two or three clean tea towels to allow the loin to rest, ideally for 1 hour before you serve. It's up to you if you like the porchetta sliced thinly or thickly.

Tip from the kitchen

To make extra gravy, remove the loin from the tray. Place the tray over a direct heat and deglaze the pan with a generous amount of white wine. Slowly simmer the juices until they have reduced by half. Sieve into a pot and leave to sit, away from the heat, to allow any fats to come to the surface. Skim them off and then return to the heat. Check the seasoning and add a little water if it's too strong.

STUFATO DI CAPRA AL PECORINO

Serves 3-4

2 large onions, peeled and cut into chunks

2 tbsp extra virgin olive oil

1kg goat or lamb shoulder cut into large chunks, preferably with the bone still on

sea salt flakes and freshly milled black pepper, to taste

2 large fennel bulbs, cut into chunks

1 fresh chilli, seeds removed

4 or 5 sprigs of fresh thyme

1 star anise (adds a little extra depth)

¼ bottle of good white wine, like Pecorino

8-10 fresh fennel fronds, stalks removed, washed and finely chopped

Capra is goat and Pecorino is sheep, but Pecorino is also a white Italian grape variety that confused the living daylights out of me when I first heard of it. Many of our French-trained team are shocked when we say we always cook lamb or goat with white wine, and even more so when we say we love to drink white wine when eating it.

This hearty roast is easy, and is delicious served with beans and Salsa di menta (p. 150). In fairness, even for us getting a goat is a challenge, so lamb would be equally delicious.

Start by softening the onions in the oil in a deep casserole and then remove. Next add the meat and brown. Season generously. Add the fennel, chilli, thyme and star anise. Add the wine and an extra few drizzles of extra virgin olive oil.

Cover and roast for 1½–2 hours in a hot oven (220°C/425°F/Gas 7) until the meat is tender.

Remove from the oven, check seasoning and add the fresh fennel fronds to finish.

Tip from the kitchen

On the Continent, meat is butchered very differently to here in Britain. Cuts that we have here, they don't have. For smaller animals like a baby goat, piglet or a lamb, the meat tends to be cut with the bone and roasted with the bones intact. If you are able to get a goat, not kidding, it's better to ask for the meat to be prepared the European way. You'll get so much more flavour. The Italian description, scottadito – 'burned fingers' – will have full effect when you get to eat the flesh from the bones.

Contorni

PUGLIA

Puglia stretches from Bari all the way down to the heel of the boot of Italy. It's one of the lesser known regions, but it's probably one of the most naturally beautiful and we love it.

The climate, food, people and architecture of this region are all strikingly Puglian. *Trulli* – tiny, idyllic, domed hobbit-style houses – can only be found here. When the children were little, we found ourselves on many beautiful holidays in a converted *masseria* (a farmhouse in the centre of a large olive grove), with every fruit tree you can imagine decorating our evening walks.

Puglia is quieter, safer, more relaxed and an escape from the busier parts of Italy. Puglia isn't our home turf but we could easily live here.

The vast majority of what is produced over the winter in Italy is grown here. We've visited our producers on many occasions and the terrain, while it looks dry and far too rugged, is rich and very generous, offering a huge wealth of fabulous food treasures. Olive trees dominate the landscape; we usually always have an olive oil from Puglia in our kitchen at George Street. It is also home to the incredibly rich, triple-cream, animal-rennet fresh cow's milk cheese loved by our customers, burrata. (I'm more of a mozzarella girl. It's no coincidence that even my palate feels that little bit more familiar slightly closer to Campania.)

While you could travel by train relatively easily between the north all the way down to

Calabria in the south, a car is really needed when in Puglia. Before the days of satnav, we got lost on many occasions. The diversity within the region means taking time to travel is essential – each town has its own character and reason to visit.

For me, the highlights include the magical hilltop town of Ostuni, with its winding medieval streets and its most famous restaurant, Osteria del Tempo Perso. Alberobello is an enchanting miniature metropolis lined with *trulli*. Add to this open-air music (in July, concerts seem to pop up out of nowhere) and I can bring back memories of my girls dancing through the streets.

Closer to Bari is Monopoli and glamorous Polignano a Mare, perched by the sea. Home to one of Europe's most famous diving competitions, this feels like the California of Italy, filled with beautiful people.

Further inland you'll come across the unique architecture of the UNESCO site of Matera, whose houses are carved into the rock. Many have been restored back to dwellings, hotels and restaurants. How lucky we are that cities like this have been salvaged for future generations.

Puglian bread is famed throughout Italy. Pane di Altamura DOP, with its thick crust, slow prove, huge air bubbles and low salt, is iconic. Add a good dunking of olive oil and it's the perfect partner for Crema di fave, my favourite Puglian dish.

CREMA DI CANNELLINI

Serves 4

500g dried cannellini beans, soaked overnight

sea salt flakes and freshly milled black pepper, to taste

extra virgin olive oil

The finished texture of cannellini beans is very similar to beautiful Puglian fave. Dried cannellini are far easier to get your hands on than fave, so I've used them. In the restaurants, we serve this as a base for grilled lamb rump, with roasted violet aubergines to add texture. Here, I've served it with Zucca con Salsa di menta (p. 150). Delicious.

Rinse and soak the dried beans overnight in three times the volume of water with a half teaspoon of bicarbonate of soda.

Rinse again and then simmer with more fresh water until they come to the boil. Rinse again to remove all of the residue of the bicarbonate of soda, then place back in the pot. Cover with at least three times the volume of water and simmer in a very low oven (130°C/265°F/Gas 1–2) for 3 hours until the beans are super soft. Never add salt while cooking, as this makes the skins tough. Strain the beans and reserve the cooking liquid.

Transfer the beans to a bowl or pot, add a ladle of the cooking liquid and a generous amount of extra virgin olive oil, then blend with a hand blender. You're looking for the texture of lightly whipped double cream. Season and serve warm with some more good olive oil to finish.

Tip from the kitchen

Chunky works, too. Once cooked, drain and add the beans to a pan in which you have already fried a very thinly sliced sweet red onion with a pinch of dried chilli. Add a little of the cooking liquid and a generous drizzle of good oil. Cook until soft and slightly emulsified. Season and enjoy.

ZUCCA
con Salsa di menta

Serves 4

750g–1kg pumpkin or squash (skin and seeds removed, sliced into wedges)

extra virgin olive oil

2 tsp aged balsamic vinegar

½ nutmeg, freshly grated

1 tbsp light runny honey

sea salt flakes, to taste

2–3 sprigs of fresh thyme, leaves only

zest of 1 unwaxed orange

For the Salsa di menta

150g fresh mint, leaves only, coarsely chopped

100g fresh parsley, leaves only, coarsely chopped

1 large garlic clove, finely chopped

1 fresh red chilli, seeds removed, finely chopped

zest of 1 unwaxed lemon

3–4 tbsp peppery extra virgin olive oil

squeeze of lemon juice

sea salt flakes, to taste

Some vegetables need a bit of a helping hand. A favourite herb can do the trick and boost their flavour. The finishing touch in my kitchen is usually citrus zest. Pumpkin often needs the most support.

Choose a large, flat baking tray and line with parchment paper.

In a bowl mix the pumpkin with the extra virgin olive oil, balsamic, nutmeg, honey and a generous sprinkle of salt. Mix well. Place on the baking tray and sprinkle the thyme on top.

Bake at 180°C/350°F/Gas 4 for 30 minutes until tender. Finish with the finely grated zest of the orange and another drizzle of oil, with a final pinch of salt.

Salsa di menta

Occasionally it's necessary to throw in a showstopper. The cannellini and the zucca are delicious together, but combining them with Salsa di menta can turn them into a special dinner.

Mix all the ingredients, and add the lemon juice and seasoning to check the flavours are balanced. Every oil will give a different taste, so the quantity of lemon and salt will very much depend on your preference.

Tip from the kitchen

Have a date night. Even after years of marriage. Could someone remind Victor, please?

VERDURE
con Burro al peperoncino

Serves 2

100g one-day-old (or two-day-old) bread, cut into chunks

25g lovage, leaves only, finely chopped

25g flat-leaf parsley, leaves only, finely chopped

few sprigs of marjoram or oregano, finely chopped

sea salt flakes, to taste

1 sweet red Italian pepper, deseeded and cubed

1 courgette, cubed

1 small violet aubergine, cubed

1 red onion, peeled and chopped

2 beetroot, peeled and cubed

extra virgin olive oil, for roasting

handful of Taggiasche olives, stones removed

For the Burro al peperoncino

100g unsalted butter

2 red chillies, cut in half and seeds removed: do not slice

sea salt flakes, to taste

The vegetables and herbs from our kitchen garden may change throughout the year, but this basic dish stays the same. The favourite combination seems to be a mixture of Italian and Scottish vegetables. Enjoy as you wish.

First, start by making the breadcrumbs. Scatter the bread on a large baking tray, drizzle with oil and roast until golden. Finely chop all the herbs and add to the breadcrumbs, then roast for a few minutes more to help dry them. Season with a little salt. Remove from the oven and allow to cool. Transfer to a food processor and blend to a fine crumb. Keep warm.

Next, roast the vegetables. Chop into roughly the same size chunks and place on a baking tray. Drizzle with extra virgin olive oil and add a generous sprinkling of salt. Bake at 180°C/350°F/Gas 4 for about 20 minutes until al dente. Mix halfway through, so they cook evenly. The colour of the beetroot gives a lovely purple tinge to the dish.

To make the Burro al peperoncino, in a small pan gently melt the butter with the chillies and add the salt. Leave to infuse for about 5 minutes. Remove the whole chillies before using.

Remove the vegetables from the oven, add the olives to warm them through and coat in chilli butter. Serve with the warm crumb scattered on top.

Tip from the kitchen

Waste not, want not. The humble loaf in its freshest form is a gift from the gods. One day old is tasty toast. A day older is brilliant bruschetta. But where are you on day four? No need to waste – it can be perfect crumbs.

MELANZANE ALLA PARMIGIANA

Serves 4

500g violet aubergines

1 serving of butter sugo (p. 79)

2 balls mozzarella, sliced and allowed to drain (if you use cow's milk mozzarella, it is more dense and less liquid, so a few minutes is enough for this; if you use mozzarella di bufala, it is creamier so you just have to leave it in a colander for about 15 minutes and dry with kitchen towel before you use it)

Parmigiano Reggiano, grated, to serve

For the béchamel

50g unsalted butter

50g plain flour

sea salt flakes and freshly milled black pepper, to taste

1 pint milk

½ nutmeg, freshly grated

This dish sounds as if it comes from Parma in the north, but its roots are very southern. Campania and Sicily claim ownership.

Violet aubergines are best in this recipe, but they are very difficult to source. The black-skinned ones can be very bitter, so it's a good idea to slice the aubergine and leave in a colander with a sprinkle of salt for about 10–15 minutes to remove the bitter juices.

You can add the mozzarella into the béchamel if you want the texture to be more like a lasagne.

To make the béchamel, melt the butter in a small saucepan and add the flour. Cook for about 3 minutes to break down the starch. Season with salt and pepper, and then, using a whisk, add the milk. Cook until the milk begins to thicken. Add the nutmeg and check the seasoning again.

Very thinly slice the aubergines, brush with extra virgin olive oil and roast on a baking tray for 10 minutes (200°C/400°F/Gas 6).

Choose a 24cm deep ceramic dish. Spread a little sugo on the bottom and then layer with aubergine. Cover with mozzarella and a generous amount of béchamel. Spoon a layer of sugo on top and then layer the aubergine again. Continue until the ingredients are used and finish the top with a layer of butter sugo

Bake at 180°C/350°F/Gas 4 for 40 minutes until piping hot. Serve with freshly grated Parmigiano.

Tip from the kitchen

Cooking should be fun. If you're tired, it's OK to have a rest or even a day off kitchen duties. A fish supper at the seaside will restore your faith in life and in cooking.

ASPARAGI

1 bunch of asparagus, stems snapped to remove the tough parts

100g stracchino or burrata

150ml double cream

50g Parmigiano Reggiano, grated

½ nutmeg, freshly grated

zest of 1 unwaxed lemon

sea salt flakes and freshly milled black pepper, to taste

The asparagus season is so short in Scotland, we eat them for the whole month of May and enjoy every mouthful. The Italian season starts earlier and we only sneak a little in of the white Venetian variety that's grown in Treviso.

———

Choose a shallow ceramic baking dish that the asparagus can be laid out in flat. Tear the stracchino or burrata and scatter over the asparagus. Pour in the cream and sprinkle with the Parmigiano Reggiano. Finish with the grated nutmeg, lemon zest and seasoning. Bake at 180°C/350°F/Gas 4 for 15 minutes until tender, golden and bubbling.

Tip from the kitchen

In Italy, you get a wish for the first of the season's produce. If nothing else, it gives you an excuse for a mindful moment. Something many of us don't allow ourselves often enough.

FRITTATA VERDE

Serves 4–6

4 courgettes, chopped into small cubes

2–3 tbsp extra virgin olive oil, for roasting and frying

12 large free-range eggs

100g fresh mint, leaves only, very finely chopped

25g fresh chives, very finely chopped

sea salt flakes and freshly milled black pepper, to taste

125g fresh ricotta

I can't imagine my day without eggs. Most mornings I start with two boiled eggs if I'm at home, or scrambled eggs made with double cream if I'm at work and enjoying breakfast at George Street. Eggs are cracking – and we use them in everything, from fresh pasta to zabaglione. But the easiest way to enjoy them is in frittata.

Roast the courgettes in the oven with a little oil until golden. Allow to cool.

In a large mixing bowl, crack the eggs, add the cooled, roasted courgettes, herbs and seasoning. Break up the ricotta with a fork and fold it into the egg mixture. You don't want it to be a smooth paste; you want a lumpy texture.

Choose a deep, non-stick frying pan, about 30cm across. Add some oil and heat until hot. Add a tablespoon of the egg mixture and move the pan to make sure it doesn't stick. Next add the remaining mixture and then lower the heat. Using a wooden spoon or spatula gently pull the mixture from the edges of the pan into the middle. Continue to do this until it begins to look dry.

This is the tricky part . . .

Place a large plate, the size of the pan, over the frittata and move over to the sink. Be very careful, as the mixture will still be a little wet and the oil will be hot, so don't burn yourself. Flip the pan over so the frittata is sitting on the plate, then carefully slide the frittata back into the pan, so it's now upside down, and return to the heat. Cook for a further 3–5 minutes until the frittata is cooked all the way through. Remove from the heat and slide the frittata onto a large plate.

Tip from the kitchen

Frittata is outside dining food. Best served at room temperature. Never hot, but occasionally cold.

SPINACI

Serves 2–3

1 garlic clove, skin removed

1 tbsp extra virgin olive oil

200g baby spinach leaves, washed (or if you're lucky, the large Italian leaf spinach which really gives the robust flavour when cooking)

50g sultanas

sea salt flakes, to taste

zest of 1 unwaxed lemon

pinch of mace

½ nutmeg, freshly grated

50g pine kernels, dry roasted in a pan until golden

freshly milled black pepper, to taste

Trying to get my children to eat greens wasn't easy. Thanks to Popeye, spinach has always been a favourite. I usually prefer raw baby spinach to cooked spinach, but this is a little different.

Lightly fry the whole clove of garlic in oil until golden. Add the spinach leaves and the sultanas. The sultanas will soak up a little of the water from the spinach – that's why I add them early on. When the leaves start to wilt, season with a little salt, the lemon zest, mace and nutmeg. Add the pine kernels. Finish with lots of fresh black pepper.

Tip from the kitchen

Nature or nurture? No – nurture nature. We only have one. In the process, risk growing old until it catches up with you, then relax and enjoy what's left.

CARCIOFI

Serves 4

4 artichokes, tough outer leaves removed and the stalk trimmed with a vegetable peeler

1 large garlic clove, skin removed and finely chopped

50g flat-leaf parsley, leaves only, finely chopped

50g fresh mint, leaves only, finely chopped

100g fresh breadcrumbs

sea salt flakes, to taste

2–3 tbsp extra virgin olive oil

I swithered whether to add an artichoke recipe to this book, as they are such a faff. I've ended up adding two (see Crudi, p. 166). It's all about the freshness and the preparation.

Cut the artichokes in half lengthways and scrape out the rough choke until you feel you are scraping the heart of the flower. Trim the green top of the remaining leaves; they will be tender when they go from green to yellow. Rub the artichokes with lemon and place them in a bowl of water to stop them discolouring. Don't be surprised at how much of the rough stalks you have to remove to reveal the treasures of this kitchen diamond.

Mix the garlic, herbs, breadcrumbs, salt and oil together.

Choose a heavy-bottomed casserole pot. Gently fry the mixture, then lower the heat. Fill each half of the artichoke with the breadcrumbs and place, filling side up, in the pot. Add a couple of tablespoons of warm water to help steam the flowers.

Cover with greaseproof paper and place the lid on the pot. Simmer very gently for about 20 minutes until tender.

Tip from the kitchen

Artichokes are part of the thistle family. Can you imagine eating a thistle? The central choke and outer leaves are spiky. An apple corer can help, but use your fingers to check the centre is smooth. By the end of an artichoke session, my hands, and especially my thumbs, look like they've been grated. I used to think of it as the price of true love. Now I've trained Victor to do it, it is indeed true love, as he knows the suffering us cooks have endured for decades.

GALLETTI

Serves 4

2 tbsp extra virgin olive oil

1 garlic clove, skin removed and left whole but slightly crushed

1 whole dried chilli

200g fresh chanterelle mushrooms, wiped with a damp cloth and any earth or grass removed

50g flat-leaf parsley, leaves only, chopped

sea salt flakes, to taste

Scotland, like Italy, has a reputation for excellent foraging. Ceps and chanterelles can be as abundant in the Highlands of Scotland as in the hills of Tuscany. Victor is a porcini man. For years, he had a picture of a perfect porcino he'd found as his screensaver. Three children and a wife, but a fungo was his favourite photo. He's a fun guy (couldn't resist). For me, chanterelles are my golden, gorgeous jewels.

Choose a large, flat frying pan and gently heat the oil. Add the garlic and fry until golden. Add the chilli and the chanterelles. Raise the heat, shake the pan and fry until the mushrooms are soft but not mushy. Add the parsley and season with salt.

They are now ready for a plethora of possibilities. These can be a topping for garlic bruschetta; they are delicious with mozzarella or burrata and more extra virgin olive oil; and are perfect with finely sliced Prosciutto di Parma, or Speck di Prosciutto, the slightly smoky variation.

Tip from the kitchen

Never pick or eat a mushroom if you aren't 100 per cent sure what it is. They can be lethal. What's the old saying? You can eat all mushrooms, but there are some you will only ever eat once. None of those ones, please.

PEPERONI

Serves 2

2 large red peppers

1 garlic clove, sliced

6 anchovies

2 sprigs of fresh oregano, leaves only

sea salt flakes, to taste

2 tbsp extra virgin olive oil

The smell of peppers roasting while they gently release their skins is happy cooking. The rich red colour alone makes you feel good when it's dreich outside.

Wipe the peppers and place them whole on a roasting tray and bake at 220°C/425°F/Gas 7 for 30 minutes or until the skins are black. Remove from the oven and carefully peel the skin from the peppers. Cut the stalk to remove the seeds. Slice the peppers into strips and place on a platter. Add the garlic, anchovies and oregano. Season with salt and dress with extra virgin olive oil. Enjoy at room temperature.

Tip from the kitchen

This dish doesn't need the anchovies. Substitute the oregano and anchovies with a teaspoon of vincotto and fresh basil leaves – whatever the mood or the company dictates.

Insalate

CRUDI

Serves 4

4 artichokes, tough outer leaves removed and the stalk trimmed with a vegetable peeler

sea salt flakes, to taste

2 tbsp extra virgin olive oil

20 fresh mint leaves, finely chopped

20 parsley leaves, finely chopped

zest and juice of 1 unwaxed lemon

100g ricotta salata

Raw salads are so refreshing and this is one of my favourite ways to eat artichokes. They have to be young, super tender and fresh. If your carciofi meets these three golden rules, you're in for a treat and this is the recipe to go for. This also works with raw courgettes, fennel, celery or the fruity tomato which we usually take for granted is raw in a salad.

The hard work is preparing the artichokes (see Carciofi, p. 159, for full instructions).

Very finely slice the cleaned artichokes, placing them in a bowl of water with a few squeezed lemon wedges to stop them discolouring.

When you're ready to assemble the salad, drain the artichokes and pat dry. Scatter them into a large salad bowl. Season with salt and dress with extra virgin olive oil.

Add the herbs, and the lemon juice and zest. Mix well. Transfer to a platter and generously shave the ricotta salata on top.

Tip from the kitchen

Music for the soul is as important as food for the body. There is always time to have a little dance, even in the kitchen.

RADICCHIO DI TREVISO

Serves 4

1 bulb of radicchio

1 pear, ripe but firm

large handful of seedless red grapes, washed and cut in half

50g hazelnuts, skins removed, toasted and roughly chopped

sea salt flakes, to taste

extra virgin olive oil

1 tbsp light honey

zest of 1 orange

There are so many combinations of good flavours, and there is no right and wrong if food is fresh and in season. Chicory can be challenging for some, as it's one of the more bitter salad leaves. Adding a sharp acid, such as lemon juice, or sweetness, from a fruit such as the pear in this recipe, tends to balance the bitterness. On the same flavour spectrum as chicory but more pronounced is the beautifully deep pink-coloured Venetian salad radicchio di Treviso, a more torpedo-shaped version of the rounder radicchio. It's often served chargrilled, which mellows the flavour.

Wash and finely slice the radicchio and place in a bowl. Chop the pear into matchsticks and scatter over the leaves. Add the grapes and hazelnuts. Season with salt, and drizzle with the oil and honey. Finish with the orange zest.

Tip from the kitchen

You are allowed to change your mind. This is the most important lesson I've learned in business. I sometimes wish I'd known it earlier, but it's never too late to learn.

ANGURIA E CAPRINO

Per person

100g fresh watermelon, deseeded and cut into chunks

75g caprino, or a young goat's cheese

4–6 basil leaves, torn

small handful of fresh mint leaves, torn

extra virgin olive oil

sea salt flakes, to taste

50g hazelnuts, roasted, skins removed, coarsely crushed

Eating in the garden in Scotland can be a rare occurrence, but when it happens it's a feast. When we buy watermelon from Italy, the average size is around 6kg and we use it largely in martinis or salads. This dish, or the seafood version (see Granchio, p. 115), is always a hit.

Eating the watermelon, chilled, outside, is a perfect way to help use up the remaining kilos.

In a salad bowl add the watermelon, caprino and herbs. Dress with extra virgin olive oil and a generous pinch of salt. Serve with the hazelnuts scattered on top.

Tip from the kitchen

As Monty Python say, 'Always look on the bright side of life.'

SICILY

We've visited Sicily several times, which still isn't enough to have a true opinion. The food, the language and the landscape – even the mindset – are very different to those on the mainland.

The little Aeolian islands scattered in the Tyrrhenian Sea are an adventure. Taking a *traghetto* there is one of the most romantic trips you can experience – the journey lasts about four hours and when timed with the sunset it is stunning.

My parents always took their holidays in Sicily in September, staying in a hotel on the beach below Taormina. I joined them in 1987, when I was in sixth year at school.

Taormina has a Roman amphitheatre, a funicular and a tourist feel, and offers a taste of relaxed, sophisticated street life. TV series *The White Lotus* gave the local San Domenico Palace Hotel the look. If you want to stay in a converted monastery in the lap of luxury, this fits the bill in every way.

Mount Etna towers above Taormina. Caltanissetta, Corleone and similar hillside towns will take you straight to *The Godfather*. The beaches are pebbly, so your feet will be polished if you can bear the torture. I never can.

Back in 1987, I arrived to be met by my father, smiling, with his pipe perched between his teeth, wearing crisp white tennis shorts, a Pringle striped polo shirt, size 48, and my grandmother's knitted socks in green wool, the same yarn for kilt socks, squeezed into his black Barbour shoes. The Hollywood glam of the 1930s and '50s was usually his style, but when it came to daytime holidaying in the heat, comfort took over. My sweetheart. I love him more for it now, but I think I changed to the colour of the lava up the hill on Etna when I saw him.

I'd never been on holiday with my parents before. Probably the result of being one of eight children. Sunday came and surprise, surprise, we were going to church. No rest for the wicked, even on holiday. Like most small towns, there is one central promenade. Five minutes into the walk, from behind me I heard, 'Carina, Carina . . .' I turned around, and guess who was in Taormina

for the day? My future husband, although he didn't know it at the time. If he did, he didn't admit it. He was apparently driving through Sicily with three of his friends. It might have taken my 'very light' slap across his cheek after an attempted sneaky kiss when I was 19, plus another two years, for him to ask me out, but Sicily will always feel like our first date.

When I think of food in Sicily, I think of rich sauces, strong flavours, seafood and cake. Garlic, pine kernels, almonds, olives, capers, rich olive oils, preserves used in multiple layers, all adding the extra levels of flavours that distinguish Sicilian cooking. Fish, as every seaside village has a fleet of little boats that keep the restaurants and locals well fed. Agrodolce, sweet and sour, is the Sicilian classic that filters through all courses and probably describes their style of cooking better than anything. The flavours of this island leave your palate challenged and excited.

Their cakes and sweet treats are wonderful. Sicilian pastry shops have a super league status all of their own. Cassata and cannoli, two pastry icons, both have ricotta as their essential ingredient. Window displays are overflowing with every shape and colour of marzipan fruits and decorations. Pastel-coloured sugared almonds are proudly displayed in large ornate glass jars, the envy of any Victorian sweet shop. Biscotti di mandorle – bite-size moreish mouthfuls made with almonds, studded with nuts or candied fruits and dusted with icing sugar – are sold in beautiful printed paper-wrapped trays with twisted ribbons as gifts for family back home. If they make it that far . . .

ARANCIA

Serves 2

2 large navel oranges, outside pith removed to the flesh and cut into circles

1 bulb fennel, trimmed and finely sliced

handful of fresh fennel fronds, stalks removed, finely chopped

handful of fresh parsley leaves, stalks removed, finely chopped

12 large green olives, stones removed and roughly chopped

sea salt flakes, to taste

glug of extra virgin olive oil

zest of 1 unwaxed lemon

splash of sambuca (optional – my brother Mark's favourite!)

Salads are seasonal and this one is far more winter than summer. The kick of vitamin C from the oranges makes you feel summer won't be long in coming. If you're able to drive around Sicily, the pockets of orange and lemon trees that constantly dot the landscape are a perfect reminder of how happy citrus fruits are on this island. In January, we're able to get blood oranges from Tarocco. The intense deep ruby colour of this super citrus makes this salad even more tantalising.

―――――

Choose a large salad platter and layer the oranges and fennel. Scatter the herbs and olives on top. Generously season with salt and dress with the oil, zest and the sambuca.

Tip from the kitchen
―――――
Never stop cuddling those you love, especially the little people. No one is ever too big for a cuddle.

ZUCCHINI

Serves 4

3 small courgettes, finely sliced

50g rocket leaves

3 courgette flowers, wiped with a damp cloth and the stamen removed

1 fresh red chilli, seeds removed, very finely chopped

sea salt flakes, to taste

extra virgin olive oil

1 unwaxed lemon

50g Parmigiano Reggiano, shaved, to serve

Our kitchen garden provides an abundance of courgettes and their flowers. Watching the leaves bud morning and evening is a delight. We grow so many, we're able to deliver twice a day to the restaurants.

Finely slice the courgettes and scatter over a large platter. Place the rocket leaves and courgette flower petals on top. Scatter the chilli over these. Season with salt and dress with the oil and lemon. Finely shave the Parmigiano on top.

Tip from the kitchen

Fresh chillies can be dangerous. Each has a different heat, so get to know the varieties and choose wisely. Most importantly, wash your hands thoroughly afterwards. The slightest trace of the capsaicin (the chemical that makes chillies hot) in your eyes can be a long-lasting sting far worse than any ouch.

MELOGRANO

Serves 4

100g young spinach leaves, washed and dried

6–8 strips of cooked Amalfi lemon (see below)

½ pomegranate, seeds only

20g sultanas, soaked in hot fresh apple juice and allowed to cool

20g blanched almonds, roasted and crushed

sea salt flakes, to taste

extra virgin olive oil

drizzle of honey

Cooked Amalfi lemons

4 unwaxed Amalfi lemons

100g caster sugar

3 bay leaves

50ml white wine vinegar

1 sprig of fresh thyme

This is a George Street staple. It is named after a hotel in Puglia that's surrounded by these beautiful pomegranate trees. So many happy memories. This salad will leave you feeling happy and healthy. It offers a fabulous taste, from start to finish.

Scatter the spinach leaves onto a large plate. Drain the sultanas. Arrange the strips of lemon, pomegranate seeds, sultanas and almonds on top. Season with salt and dress with oil and a drizzle of honey.

Cooked Amalfi lemons

The Amalfi lemon season is from February to October. Over the winter months we buy from further south, in Puglia, but the sweetness of the skins and the flesh isn't as luscious as in the traditional Amalfi variety. The tradition of preserving lemons in salt lies on the other side of the Mediterranean in Morocco, so we developed a recipe that allows us to get a better flavour from the fruit out of season. The great benefit is that these can be made in a day rather than over months, and they last for about a week.

Wash the lemons, then place all the ingredients in a small pot and cover with just enough cold water. Bring to the boil, lower the heat, cover with greaseproof paper and place a lid on top. Gently simmer for about 40 minutes until the lemons are soft. Remove from the heat and allow to cool in the liquid. Save the cooking brine.

Trim the ends of the fruit and cut the lemons in half. Remove the pulp and slice the skin into finger-length strips. Store the strips in the cooking brine in a sterilised Kilner jar in the fridge for up to a week.

The pulp is delicious in a salad dressing, with some spicy extra virgin olive oil and a little salt. Pass it through a fine sieve and store in the fridge for 2 or 3 days.

Tip from the kitchen

Tradition in cooking is my essential ingredient. Without tradition, I'd miss far too many chapters and all the learning along the way.

FAVE

100g Prosciutto di Parma or sliced pancetta affumicata

1 small lettuce, such as a frisse or cos, washed and dried

1kg (un-podded weight) fresh broad beans, podded and skinned

100g blanched almonds, roasted and roughly chopped

20 or so mint leaves

sea salt flakes, to taste

2 tbsp extra virgin olive oil

1–2 tsp aged balsamic vinegar

few shavings of Parmigiano Reggiano (optional)

#NoFavourites – this is what I tell my team (and my children). But I adore the fresh broad bean season. Nature doesn't always make life easy. It takes time to pod these beauties, but also to peel them. The thick skin that sits over the two halves has to be removed. I find this task almost therapeutic. You can lose hours in meditation, podding broad beans. I've always preferred tasks like this to going to the gym.

Layer the Prosciutto or pancetta on a baking sheet and bake in a hot oven for about 10 minutes. You want this to be crisp, so that it snaps when it's cool.

Place the salad leaves in a large salad bowl. Add the broad beans and almonds. Tear the mint leaves and snap the Prosciutto into pieces, and add these to the salad. Season and then dress with the oil and balsamic vinegar.

I'm a sucker for Parmigiano. You can add some shavings to make this even more moreish.

Tip from the kitchen

Slowing down does sometimes get you to where you want to go quicker.

PUNTARELLE
con Salsa di acciughe

1 young puntarelle, outer bitter leaves removed

For the Salsa di acciughe

1 garlic clove

3 anchovies in oil

3–4 tbsp extra virgin olive oil

1 fresh red chilli, seeds removed, very finely sliced

small handful of flat-leaf parsley, leaves only, chopped

1 dessertspoon of red wine vinegar

¼ tsp sea salt flakes

There are some ingredients that just say Italy. Puntarelle is one of them. I've seen it in some top-end delis, for sure, when in season, and definitely in some classy Italian restaurants, but never in a supermarket in Britain. It's a cross between fennel and celery. It has beautiful, almost triffid-like outer leaves that are very bitter, but the younger, more tender ones can be used in soups. The beauty is the heart. The trick is how to cut these little fingers and the secret is to do so as finely, and as long and thinly, as possible.

I feel about truffles how some people feel about anchovies. The smell alone makes me recoil into my PJs. My safe space. For those who love anchovies, like me, Salsa di acciughe is heaven. Perfect with steak, fish and almost everything else. I hear you say, the same could apply to truffles . . .

If you can't get puntarelle, the Salsa di acciughe dressing works very well with chicory or fennel.

First, prepare the puntarelle. Have a large bowl of ice-cold water nearby, with a lemon cut into quarters and placed in the water. This stops the leaves from discolouring. Keep any of the very short leaves and add to the iced water. Break off the fingers (for want of a better word) of the bulb of the puntarella and cut them in half on a chopping board. Cut the fingers into as many long, thin strips as you can. Add to the iced water and continue until the bulb has been cut.

To make the Salsa di acciughe, use a pestle and mortar to cream the garlic and anchovies until smooth. Slowly add the olive oil and then fold in the chilli, parsley and vinegar. Check for seasoning and add the salt if required. Sometimes the anchovy is particularly salty, so add sparingly.

When you are ready to assemble the dish, rinse the puntarelle under the cold tap, drain and dry it with kitchen roll. These little strips will naturally curl in the water and this is the look you want, as it helps the Salsa di acciughe to stick. Serve immediately. The crisp, cold puntarelle makes this salad so refreshing.

Tip from the kitchen

Old (or last season's) garlic can be very pungent and quite heady. Don't be tempted to always use the full amount in any recipe. The smell of the garlic alone should be enough for you to gauge how much you need. Less is, in the case of garlic, usually better.

CAVOLFIORE

Serves 4

1 small cauliflower

sea salt flakes, to taste

juice of 1 unwaxed lemon

extra virgin olive oil

10 dried figs, finely sliced

50g Venetian honey walnuts (see Noci con Miele, p. 50), slightly crushed

This salad is a triumph in the winter when you're looking for something refreshing but with a bit of heartiness. It's a raw salad, so make sure your cauliflower is super fresh. Our family in Italy sometimes share their homegrown and handmade sun-dried figs. If you receive these in the post, you're clearly loved.

Wash the cauliflower and shake dry. Using a mandoline (or the cutting blade on a food processor), thinly slice the cauliflower. Place in a salad bowl. Season and dress with lemon juice and oil. Decorate with the figs and walnuts.

Tip from the kitchen

Fresh walnuts in winter are by far the best. They are a faff to open and are best roasted in a dry frying pan. If you are using packet walnuts, always check they are not rancid.

MOZZARELLA DI BUFALA

We're fanatical about mozzarella. Victor's father taught him well. Mozzarella and Nonno Carlo both came from Campania, just outside of Naples, where the water buffaloes graze on the very fertile soil within sight of Mount Vesuvius. The training has rubbed off on me, too. This cheese is classically served with tomatoes – the most famous are the San Marzano that are grown on the slopes of this ancient volcano – and basil leaves: the iconic Caprese salad that showcases the colours of the Italian flag.

Substitute the tomatoes for fresh apricots, peaches or – even better – fresh figs and the excitement and flavour levels fly even higher.

No recipe is required: just use fresh, simple Italian ingredients dressed with an olive oil from any region near Campania, with a little seasoning. Tre colori combinations on full display.

Tip from the kitchen

Should we teach our children to be self-sufficient or keep them as protected from the real world as possible? We went for the former. Time will tell, but it's looking good so far.

PANZANELLA

Serves 4

250g baby plum tomatoes, cut in half

250g baby yellow plum tomatoes, cut in half

1 cucumber, cut in half lengthwise, seeds removed and sliced at an angle into thin wedges

20 fresh basil leaves

20 flat-leaf parsley leaves

1 small salad onion, peeled, finely sliced and left to soak in cold water for about 5 minutes

20 Taggiasche olives, pitted

100g day-old bread, cut into chunks and lightly fried in a little olive oil until golden

2 anchovies (optional), cut very finely

sea salt flakes, to taste

extra virgin olive oil, for the dressing

1 tbsp red wine vinegar, to taste

This classic salad is a meal in itself.

Once you have prepared all of the ingredients, mix them together. Season and dress with the oil and vinegar, to taste.

This salad is often better when the bread has had a chance to soak up the juices, so make it and eat it within a half-hour or so.

Tip from the kitchen

'Taste testers' are essential in any kitchen. Best put to work before the food is served.

Dolci

MACEDONIA
con Sorbetto al limone

Serves 2

200g ripe black cherries

2 ripe yellow or white flesh peaches

your favourite type of sweet melon – I love orange cantaloupe

handful of wild strawberries (if you can get your hands on these you've won the lottery – we've got quite a few in our kitchen garden that peek out from nowhere every so often in the summer); small Scottish strawberries will work just as well

1 tsp icing sugar

2–3 tbsp Maraschino liqueur (optional), or freshly squeezed orange juice

For the Sorbetto al limone

250ml water

250g caster sugar

zest of 2 unwaxed lemons

125ml lemon juice

Fruit salad can be made with anything, but for me this is everything I love about Italy in a bowl. Colourful, vibrant and as close to a Dolce & Gabbana Smeg kitchen as I will get.

———

Wash the cherries, cut in half and remove the stone. Wash, peel and de-stone the peaches, and cut into chunks. Deseed the melon and cut into small chunks. Add the strawberries.

Dust with the icing sugar and add the Maraschino liqueur (a delicious lightly fruity Italian liquor made from cherries), then leave in the fridge for about 1 hour.

Enjoy freshly chilled from the fridge on its own, or with some homemade Amalfi lemon sorbetto (see below).

Sorbetto al limone

We're taken to the Amalfi coast every Monday, when wooden crates of fragrant, huge Amalfi lemons arrive, their crisp green leaves poking out of the boxes. If you visit Amalfi in the summer, street vendors sell these gorgeous lemons filled with frozen sorbet. Beautiful.

———

Heat the water, sugar and lemon zest in a pan. Bring to the boil and simmer for a few minutes until it starts to ever so slightly thicken. Remove from the heat and allow to cool. Add the lemon juice and then pass through a sieve. Transfer to a clean plastic container and freeze for 1 hour. Remove and beat with a mixer for a few minutes to break up the ice crystals. Return to the freezer for another hour, then remove and beat again to break up the crystals. Do this every hour three or four more times until the texture is smooth like ice cream. Ideally, if you have a fancy ice-cream freezing machine at home, this will do the work for you.

Tip from the kitchen

If in doubt, ask yourself, what would the person I'm thinking of do? You'll have your answer.

TORTA DI FICHI E MANDORLE

Serves 6

For the pastry

250g plain flour

pinch of salt

120g unsalted butter

2 free-range egg yolks

70g icing sugar

squeeze of lemon juice

For the filling

200g blanched whole almonds

200g unsalted butter at room temperature

200g golden caster

1 tsp vanilla extract

1 free-range egg

6–8 fresh figs

We love tarts and there is none better than one with nuts and fresh figs. Sticky and rich and packed with butter, it is a far more northern indulgence than anything you'd find down south. This works with any soft fruits, especially figs, peaches or apricots.

Sieve the flour and salt into a bowl. Grate the butter into the flour and mix with your fingertips to a fine breadcrumb consistency. Add the egg yolks, icing sugar and lemon juice. Combine to form a dough.

Chill for about 1 hour, then remove from the fridge and allow to come to room temperature.

Roll the pastry and line a 24cm loose-bottom deepish tart tin. Transfer back to the fridge for about 1 hour to stop the pastry from shrinking when you bake it. You don't need to par-bake this pastry.

For the filling, place the almonds on a non-stick baking tray and bake in a moderate oven until golden. Set aside and allow to cool. In a processor, blend the almonds until fine and add the butter, sugar and vanilla extract, then slowly fold in the egg. If you beat in the egg, the mixture will be too aerated and will overcook in the oven. Spoon the almond mixture on top of the pastry.

Cut the figs in half, removing the hard part of the stem. Decorate, flesh side up, on top of the almond mixture.

Transfer to a flat tray and bake in the oven (180°C/350°F/Gas 4) for 35 minutes until golden. If the top starts to brown too much and the mixture is still raw, cover with greaseproof paper and bake for another 5 or 10 minutes.

There is a lot of butter in this recipe, so don't worry if it looks runny; it's super creamy when set.

Remove from the oven and cool for a few minutes, then release the tart from the tin. Serve at room temperature with some crème fraîche or mascarpone.

Tip from the kitchen

Eat cake. Life is too short. If you cook from the heart, the food will taste better too.

TORTA DI PISTACCHIO
con Sciroppo di arancia e zafferano

Serves 6

225g unsalted butter (or 180ml olive oil, for a dairy-free alternative)

225g golden caster sugar

125g bramata polenta

225g whole blanched pistachios, roasted and ground

3 large free-range eggs

zest of 3 oranges

pinch of salt

1 tsp baking powder

For the Sciroppo di arancia e zafferano

150g caster sugar

100g water

100g orange juice

100g lemon juice

pinch of saffron

The colour of this cake alone makes it look interesting. Perfect served with a little crème fraîche. (I actually love all cakes with crème fraîche – proof, maybe, I'm not Italian after all.)

Saffron is an acquired flavour and the addition of this syrup makes this cake intriguing. It has a real taste of the Renaissance about it.

Line a 24cm deep cake tin with greaseproof paper. Set the oven to 160°C/325°F/Gas 3.

Beat the butter and sugar until light and fluffy. Gradually fold in the polenta and the ground pistachios, and alternate with the eggs. Finally fold in the zest, salt and baking powder. If the mixture seems dry, add a tablespoon of milk.

If you are using olive oil for a dairy-free version of this recipe, beat the eggs and sugar until thick and fluffy, then fold in the remaining ingredients, starting with the polenta, zest, baking powder and salt, then, finally, slowly fold in the oil.

Bake for 35–40 minutes until golden.

Meanwhile, make the Sciroppo di arancia e zafferano by simmering the sugar, water, orange and lemon juices and saffron until reduced by half. Strain to remove the saffron. Once cooled, the syrup becomes thick and glossy.

Remove the cake from the oven when cooked through. Brush a little of the syrup over the cake.

Enjoy while still warm, but not hot, with an extra drizzle of syrup on the side.

Tip from the kitchen

When baking, it's vital to have all the ingredients weighed out and ready before you start. There is nothing worse than doing the washing up and realising you've forgotten to put the eggs in the cake. The more confident the cook you are, the more disciplined you need to be. You can hear the sigh from me . . . Guilty.

CASSATA

Serves 6

For the Genovese sponge

3 large free-range eggs

200g caster sugar

175g self-raising flour

For the filling

750g fresh ricotta (Errington's fresh ewe's milk ricotta, which we get in the summer, is my ultimate ricotta)

75g icing sugar

50g fresh candied angelica, coarsely chopped

80g quality candied orange and lemon, coarsely chopped

50g quality chocolate chips (70% cocoa) – a bar of quality chocolate coarsely cut with a knife works as well, if not better

zest of 1 unwaxed orange

80g glacé, un-dyed cherries, coarsely chopped

4 tbsp Maraschino liqueur

Tip from the kitchen

This recipe really needs the Maraschino liqueur. Don't tackle it unless you've been able to source some. The flavour is iconic and really makes a very simple dessert very special.

A trip to a pasticceria in any of the major Italian cities or towns will present you with an array of deliciousness. If you're heading to Sicily, this is where you'll find the best cassata. And yes, it's a cake not an ice cream. The ice-cream variety, which will appear in most gelaterie wherever you are, and which I not surprisingly love as well, is a vanilla- or ricotta-based gelato, with the same candied fruits and chocolate chips mixed through. The cake version is made as follows.

To make the sponge, cream together the eggs and sugar until they are fluffy, with a light yellow colour.

Sieve the flour into the egg and sugar mixture and very gently fold together until smooth. It should be light and fluffy.

Transfer the mixture to a lined 20cm cake tin and bake at 180°C/350°F/Gas 4 for approximately 30 minutes until golden but not brown. Allow to cool.

The sponge should be quite deep when it comes out of the oven, but it will collapse slightly. Don't worry. Once cooled, using a large, serrated, sharp bread knife, cut through the sponge horizontally so you are left with three thin sponge layers. If you don't feel confident, two layers works equally well.

For the filling, lightly beat the ricotta and half the icing sugar until smooth. Check the sweetness and add more sugar if you like.

Fold in the angelica, candied orange and lemon, chocolate chips and the orange zest. Fold in the cherries slowly, making sure not to burst them, as their juices can change the colour of the mixture.

Choose a large cake plate and place the first slice of sponge on it. Drizzle a tablespoon of Maraschino onto the sponge, then spread over a third of the filling mixture. Repeat with the next layer of sponge: drizzle with maraschino, then spread over the ricotta, and add a final layer of sponge. Gently spread the remaining ricotta over the cake and its sides. A palette knife dipped in boiling water will help smooth the ricotta.

For the Marzipan

250g icing sugar

250g ground almonds

½ tsp almond extract

½ tsp natural green food colouring (or substitute pistachios instead of the almonds and no need for the food colouring)

100ml milk (you may not need all of this)

Alternatively, you can assemble the cake back inside the cake tin when the layers are filled, and then chill for about an hour, before removing it from the tin and spreading the remaining ricotta over the cake.

Finally roll out a layer of marzipan (see recipe below), cut a circle the same size as the cake tin and place it on top of the cake.

Refrigerate for an hour or so for the flavours to mellow together. Enough time to tidy up and get the Moka pot on. The Moka pot is Italy's original coffee pot. We once had a ski instructor in Madonna della Campagna who was the granddaughter of the inventor, Luigi di Ponti. Fun fact.

Marzipan

Walking into a pasticceria is as much fun as walking into a Gucci boutique for us Continis. I love marzipan as a finishing touch to a dessert. Painted fruit shapes don't get my tummy as excited, but they do look beautiful.

Combine the sugar, almonds, almond extract and colouring, adding the milk a little at a time to bind the mixture. Gently knead to make a light dough. Leave at room temperature until you need to dress the cake.

TIRAMISÙ

Serves 6

Genovese sponge, as per recipe on page 192

For the filling

6 large free-range eggs, separated

75g caster sugar

500g mascarpone

300ml espresso coffee

100ml Marsala all'uovo

20g dark cocoa powder, to decorate

Tip from the kitchen

Have you told anyone you love them today? It's not too late.

I honestly can't remember a day when we haven't had tiramisù on the menu at George Street. The restaurant opened in 2004 and my youngest daughter was born in 2005. Said youngest daughter went on a school trip to Sorrento when she was 11 and came back raving about this new and delicious dessert she had tried. Her friends didn't really like it, as it had a coffee flavour, so she'd got to eat theirs too. How lucky . . .

I wondered what this new and delicious discovery could be? Well, now I know why it's called 'Pick me up', as you could have picked Arianna up when I served her a portion. It had literally been under her nose the whole time at Contini George Street, but she had never wanted to even read the name, never mind give it a try.

Never one to make life easy for our team, we use homemade Genovese sponge for our tiramisù. Yes, you can use the traditional packets of Savoiardi sponge fingers at home, but in the restaurant this takes it to another level.

Once you have prepared the sponge and let it cool, start the filling.

Whisk the egg yolks with the sugar until pale and light. Add the mascarpone and mix until it starts to thicken. In a separate bowl, beat the egg whites until stiff. Gently fold them into the mascarpone mixture and set aside.

To assemble the tiramisù, start by choosing one of your prettiest dishes, as this is always best served at the table. About 20cm wide by 10cm deep will do. Cut the sponge into large slices. You'll be using two layers of sponge, so have the pieces in whatever size is comfortable for you to manage. Layer a third of the egg mixture at the bottom of the dish.

Place the espresso and the Marsala in a bowl and carefully dip the pieces of sponge in the coffee mixture, then place on top of the egg mixture in your pretty bowl. Add another layer of the egg mixture and repeat with the remaining soaked sponge. Top the dish with the remaining egg mixture, cover and refrigerate overnight to allow all the flavours to settle.

Remove from the fridge about 30 minutes before you serve and dust with the cocoa powder.

PANNA COTTA
al Caramello

Serves 6

4 gold grade gelatine leaves

1 litre single cream

1 vanilla pod, cut in half to release the seeds

140g caster sugar

For the Caramello

600g granulated sugar

600ml water

Panna cotta is as Italian as Michelangelo. We sometimes use double cream instead of single cream to take it to Sistine Chapel levels. As I've got older, I've moved back to single cream, as it's more sloppy-floppy rather than set-wobbly. This recipe is for single cream. If you need a sugar hit, caramel is my favourite topping. Simple but perfect. For something with a little sharpness, then any fruits simmered to a light compote work. Apricots or cherries are good.

Soak the gelatine leaves in cold water until soft.

Bring the cream, vanilla pod and sugar to steaming point, but don't let it boil. Remove from the heat. Squeeze any water from the soaked gelatine and add the gelatine to the cream mixture. Mix until the gelatine has melted, then strain over a sieve set over a large jug or bowl. It's important to sieve the mixture, as it catches any of the gelatine that hasn't dissolved completely. Pour into the moulds and refrigerate until set. This will take about 3 hours.

To make the Caramello, in a metal saucepan gently simmer half the sugar (300g) and half the water (300ml) until it starts to colour. This will take about 10 minutes. Stir occasionally.

In a separate pan, simmer the remaining amounts until the sugar melts. As the syrup turns a golden brown colour, remove from the heat and slowly add to the other syrup, stir and allow to cool.

To serve, dip the bottom of each mould into a bowl of hot water and then turn the contents onto a plate. It will need a wee shake, but it will come out on its own.

Serve with the caramel sauce.

Tip from the kitchen

Don't store the syrup in the fridge, as it will crystallise.

PANETTONE PUDDING
con Crema di arancia

Serves 4

For the Crema di arancia

2 free-range eggs

2 free-range egg yolks

120g caster sugar

200ml juice from about 4 blood oranges

squeeze of lemon juice

80g unsalted butter, cut into cubes

25g butter, to grease the dish

400g panettone

3 large free-range eggs

25g golden caster sugar

100ml whole milk

450ml double cream

Tip from the kitchen

The cook in our house doesn't do the dishes. Works for me. More importantly, be patient. I'm the most impatient person in the world sometimes, so I'm constantly reminding myself. It's a lesson I really should learn fast.

There is never any leftover panettone in our house, but in the restaurant we buy extra just to make this pudding. Panettone, the ubiquitous Italian Christmas cake, believed to have been invented by Antonio (translated, it's 'Tony's bread'), a junior baker, to woo his boss for permission to date his daughter. A classic Italian love story – food and destiny and a dynasty all summed up in a cake.

The addition of orange curd feels like a cuddle from your favourite Nonna – extra special. Blood oranges are in season at the start of the year, from late January through to early March. Our artisan panettone are usually out of date by the end of April, so this is good timing on both counts. The colour of the orange juice is stunning and it makes this lovely orange curd even more luxurious. If blood oranges aren't in season, any orange or lemon will do.

Start with the Crema di arancia. Mix the eggs, egg yolks, sugar and fruit juices in a glass bowl. Place this bowl over a bain-marie, ensuring the bottom doesn't touch the simmering water. Beat until the mixture starts to thicken. Slowly add the butter, one cube at a time, adding more butter as the last one melts, whisking until all the butter has been incorporated. The mixture is ready when it is thick enough to coat the back of a spoon. Allow to cool and refrigerate until you are ready to use.

To assemble the pudding, generously butter a ceramic baking dish that is about 30cm x 20cm. Slice the panettone into 1–2cm thick slices.

Mix the eggs, sugar, milk and cream together in a jug.

Layer the panettone in the ceramic dish and add a generous teaspoon of the orange curd between each piece of panettone.

Gently press the panettone down, so the curd sticks to the bread, then pour the egg mixture over the top. Leave it to soak in for about 10 minutes, then bake at 200°C/400°F/Gas 6 for 30–40 minutes until golden and slightly crispy.

Serve hot, with chilled pouring cream.

LOMBARDIA / TRENTINO–ALTO ADIGE / SÜDTIROL

The market in Milan is where we buy our weekly Italian vegetables and fruit. We've done this since day one of opening at George Street. I exaggerate by saying 'we' – this is definitely Victor's area of expertise. The largest market in Europe, like a Milan fashion warehouse for cooks, it is inspiring and vast.

We have visited many times, but the trip I remember the most is when No. 1 son was in his pram and I was pregnant with No. 2, six months before we opened the restaurant. Milan's cathedral is beautiful, but the piazza surrounding it holds one of my favourite memories: our wee boy chasing pigeons while I'm running after him with my precious bump.

Today, thanks to WhatsApp, Victor buys produce by phone. It's fast and efficient, and even during lockdown we didn't miss a delivery. With modern technology, there is no need to fly to Malpensa or Linate to place our order. This means we miss out on the stopover in the northern capital.

Milan is the home of aperitivi. Camparino, the Campari bar in the Galleria, is regarded as one of the best in the world. If you're looking for the perfect Negroni, look no further.

Other than work, the attraction of flying to Milan was that it allowed us to go further north for crisp white snow, crystal clear fresh air and a week's worth of exercise. Skiing in the Dolomites or Südtirol is special. I'm an amateur, but I love that feeling of being on top of the world, seeing nothing in front of you but the colours of my favourite dining-room china: crisp white and pure blue.

If you're not a skier but love walking, the northern lakes fall into Lombardia. Gorgeous Como is less than a 30-minute drive from Milan (or am I talking about Gorgeous George (Clooney), one of its famous residents?). This majestic lake was part of the Grand Tour of the eighteenth and nineteenth centuries. Villa del Balbianello, with its 300 years of gardens, is breathtaking. You could easily get carried away daydreaming of beautiful things (and George) across the water.

Lake Garda contains several islands, one where St Francis founded a monastery. You're surrounded by snow-capped mountains rising on

all sides. The trip around the lake, like many Italian roads, is chiselled with tunnels carved through the mountains. You can drive for hours in the dark; the children always loved guessing when we would be back in the daylight.

The lakes are definitely for those looking for tranquillity and repose, something we didn't want in our youth but which sounds more attractive as we get older.

All great food nations have different food cultures. France may try to claim the culinary crown, but I'm biased and Italy wins hands down. The Austrian influence in the border regions for food and language is unmistakable. When you visit Südtirol it becomes even more evident. In 1919, after the First World War, part of the Austro-Hungarian Empire was annexed to Italy, allowing Italy access to the Alps through the Brenner Pass. Families became Italian overnight, but one hundred years later Austrian will still be their first language and their cooking still has the flavours of schnitzel and strudel. We've only ever visited during late winter or very early spring, when there is still enough snow. The air and the mountains, not to mention the vin brulé and the bombardinos, are calling me. Lombardia these days is calling me to La Scala Milano for a favourite opera or ballet. Far safer at my age, for sure.

STRUDEL

Serves 6

For the filling

800g cooking apples, peeled and cored and cut into small, thin triangles

120g golden caster sugar

100g sultanas

1 tsp ground cinnamon

zest and juice of 1 unwaxed lemon

1 tsp vanilla extract

50g pine kernels, toasted (optional)

6 sheets of filo pastry

100g unsalted butter, melted, to brush the filo

1 free-range egg, to glaze

icing sugar, to dust on top

Tip from the kitchen

Go on, have a second portion of pudding, but go for a walk afterwards and don't have any dessert the next day. It may not make a difference to your waistline, but the fresh air will definitely do you good. My children said the other day that I always have two slices of cake, a thick one and a thin one. I must have thought the second didn't count, as I hadn't even noticed. The habit, not the consequences.

Strudel makes me think of the mountains of the northern regions of Italy. I've never been to Austria, other than flying to Innsbruck to head to the Alps, but I've been to Südtirol many times, and when you speak to the locals they are far more Austrian than Italian. While a post-war treaty may change a boundary, it can't change its people or its cooking. Thankfully, Italy has a few other recipes it can claim to be its own. Strudel has to be one of the best Austrian desserts, but when you're eating it on Italian soil it's definitely a dolce vita dessert. Now, I've not mastered the traditional strudel dough, but using filo has no boundaries.

The pine kernels are a traditional Italian addition. In Austria, I believe they tend to use chopped almonds. But you can easily leave them out if there are any nut allergies in your household. One of our family has had some very serious reactions to pine nuts over the years and it makes me slightly nervous when I'm cooking for him. It tastes just as good without.

Make the filling first. Place the apples and sugar in a saucepan with a tablespoon of water and gently steam to slightly soften the fruit. You don't want them to cook to a puree. Add the remaining filling ingredients, including the pine nuts, if you are using them, and remove from the heat. Set aside.

Heat the oven to 200°C/400°F/Gas 6. On a large work surface, lay down the first sheet of filo. Brush with butter and place another sheet on top. Continue until all the sheets have been used. Next, generously spoon the apple mixture on top of the pastry. You need to leave enough space around the edges to be able to fold them over and wrap the strudel. Use more butter when you fold the edges onto the filling, and then gently roll, so the strudel is as long as possible.

Carefully transfer to a baking sheet lined with parchment paper. Brush with egg and bake for 20–25 minutes until golden and crispy. Remove from the oven and allow to cool slightly.

This is best served warm, with some lightly whipped cream and a generous dusting of icing sugar.

ZABAGLIONE

Serves 2

4 large free-range egg yolks at room temperature

50g caster sugar

100ml Marsala all'uovo dolce

Zabaglione is one of those recipes you can keep up your sleeve and whip out from almost nowhere.

The Marsala dolce is 15% ABV, while the more aged varieties tend to be much drier and stronger, starting from 18% alcohol. For me the all'uovo dolce variety is the most palatable for most tastes.

For this recipe, you need a double boiler. A pot with a glass bowl is a great alternative; you just need to ensure that the water in the simmering pot doesn't touch the glass bowl. We've got a copper pot that we've had for years that we use just for zabaglione. It's got a round bottom – the best shape clearly for a bottom – which speeds up the process.

First, whip the egg yolks and sugar until thick and creamy.

Next, place some water in a pan on the heat. When it comes to a simmer, place the bowl with the egg yolk mixture on top. Be careful of the steam, as it could burn you.

Slowly beat the Marsala into the egg mixture. It will start to foam, but it will take about 5 or 10 minutes to thicken, depending on how good your wrist action is and how good the glass bowl or copper pan is.

You can use an electric mixer. We don't have a socket next to our cooker, so it's manual labour for us. The zabaglione is ready when the mixture has a soft, mayonnaise texture.

Serve in pretty glasses with fancy biscuits.

Tip from the kitchen

Don't eat zabaglione and drive. You'll never convince the officer you just had a dessert. It's potent. It's also delicious made with whisky or rum, for an even more punchy pudding.

TORTA AL CIOCCOLATO

Serves 6

275g caster sugar

150ml water

340g quality chocolate (70% cocoa), cut into small pieces

225g unsalted butter, at room temperature

5 large free-range eggs

Night-time is definitely for gelato and daytime is for cake. That *passeggiata* – the essential afternoon walk after a brief siesta, while it's still hot, but not too hot, and you're bored of sitting beside the pool or you're touristed out – is cake time. We very rarely have dessert in a restaurant, as we've had our cake and eaten it in the afternoon. Here in Scotland it's a whole other story and we love pudding after dinner. This is everyone's favourite.

You'll need a 25cm cake tin lined with greaseproof paper (don't use a loose-bottom one, as the cake will spoil when placed in the bain-marie).

Heat the sugar with the water until the sugar has dissolved. Add the chocolate and the butter, and once the chocolate has fully melted remove from the heat.

In a separate bowl, beat the eggs until fluffy. Very slowly add the chocolate mixture to the eggs and beat for about 10–15 minutes until thick. Pour into the lined baking tin and place in a larger, deeper tray to form a bain-marie.

Fill the tray around the tin three-quarters full with warm water. Bake at 160°C/325°F/Gas 3 for 30–40 minutes until set. Check after 25 minutes. If the top of the cake starts to look too biscuity, cover with a sheet of baking paper and continue to cook.

Remove from the oven and allow to cool in the bain-marie. Once completely cold, remove from the tin and serve at room temperature with crème fraîche.

Tip from the kitchen

Having run restaurants for more than 20 years, I have seen the number of allergies and dietary requirements increase dramatically over time. I'm not sure where this is heading. Time will tell. Choice diets are very different to allergies. Having had young children with many different allergies, I'm very aware of the responsibility and need for awareness. This wheat-free cake has been a winner for many gluten intolerance and coeliac sufferers.

Pane, Torte & Biscotti

FOCACCIA
con Salsa di pomodoro

400ml warm water

15g fresh (or 7g dried) yeast

1 tsp sugar

700g strong white flour

15g salt

2–4 tbsp extra virgin olive oil

2 sprigs of fresh rosemary, stalks removed and very finely chopped

sea salt flakes, to taste

Other additional toppings:

1 large onion, peeled and finely sliced

1 large waxy potato, cooked and thinly sliced

100g seedless grapes, cut in half

For the Salsa di pomodoro

250g semi-dried tomatoes in oil

1 garlic clove

10g fresh basil, leaves only

½ tsp dried oregano

extra virgin olive oil

Tip from the kitchen

If your yeast is old, your flour is out of date or your kitchen is cold, you'll never make any type of bread. Fresh and cosy will get you all light and fluffy. Dried yeast is often easier to get your hands on, but make sure it's in date and use half the weight as that stated for fresh yeast.

When we had the pizza oven at George Street, we were able to make a very thin, soft pizza-style focaccia. It was loved, and there are some customers who still haven't forgiven us for taking it away. The cost of the annual painting of our 18-foot-high ceilings sadly put a stop to the pizza. Without a pizza oven, we make focaccia in the pastry oven. Different equipment really is needed for different dishes.

This focaccia recipe works in a traditional convection oven, so everyone should be able to bake it at home. Focaccia is made all over Italy. In Puglia, they add mashed potato. The thinnest version comes from Liguria. I like ours thick, like my skin.

Mix the water, yeast and sugar together and let it foam. Warm the flour in the mixing bowl in the oven and then add the salt and yeast. Mix with the dough hook for about 10–15 minutes until it is elastic. Cover the bowl with cling film and leave in a warm part of your kitchen for about 30 minutes to 1 hour until it has doubled in size.

Transfer the dough onto a floured surface and gently knock it back. Lightly grease a 3cm-deep 30cm square baking tray and transfer the dough into the tray. Make holes in the dough with your fingers. Cover and allow to prove for another 30 minutes to 1 hour until it has doubled in size again. Remove the cover and generously drizzle with more oil. Gently squeeze the rosemary down into the dough. Season and set aside.

Bake in a hot oven (190°C/375°F/Gas 5) for 25 minutes until the dough is crispy on top but spongy and cooked in the middle.

Salsa di pomodoro

We serve Sofia's Olive Oil – or a new season Tuscan extra virgin olive oil, when we can get our hands on it – with the focaccia. When we can't, this is delicious for dipping.

Blend the tomatoes, garlic, basil and oregano together on a low speed in a food processor or liquidiser. The mixture should be a smoothish paste. Thin it down with extra oil.

PIZZA AL TAGLIO

1½ tins (600g) Italian plum tomatoes

2 tbsp extra virgin olive oil (one from Lazio or Campania will be fruity)

1 tsp dried oregano

1 garlic clove, peeled and sliced in half

2 tsp sea salt flakes

Pizza dough

Makes 2 small trays

700g 00 bread flour

14g fresh (or 7g dried) yeast

1 tsp caster sugar

500ml hand hot water

3 tsp table salt

I don't know if Nonna Olivia, Victor's lovely mummy, had a hidden agenda. I can remember every time I visited my then 'Aunty Olive', when I was in my teenage years, being greeted with the smell of homemade pizza. The smell of love. I loved her son, but if this was a tactic to fall in love with the mother-in-law too – it worked.

When we make pizza at home, it's not the same as pizza in a pizzeria. The dough is thicker and we rarely use cheese as a topping. Anchovies (yes, those little devils), slices of spicy Italian sausage, thinly sliced onions and red peppers, but rarely cheese.

This is the salsa we use. It's slightly chunky and tasty. Cheese isn't really needed.

Chop the tomatoes into small pieces and place with the sauce into a bowl.

Add the extra virgin olive oil, oregano and the garlic. Add the salt and check the flavour. It's interesting how much salt tomato takes to balance the acidity.

Pizza dough

Sieve the flour into a large bowl. Leave to warm in a simmering oven (or airing cupboard – I've also used the tumble dryer in the past). In a glass jug, mix the yeast and sugar with the water. If using fresh yeast, make sure the jug has enough space for the water to bubble and ferment. Cover with cling film and leave in a warm place for about 15 minutes.

Remove the bowl of flour from the oven and add the salt. Make sure it's not too hot, as this will kill the yeast and the dough won't rise.

Remove the cling film from the yeast mixture and stir. If the yeast is fresh, it will foam and fizz when you mix it. Add the yeast to the flour. I tend to place the bowl in the sink and mix by hand until a dough starts to form.

Transfer to a floured surface and knead for about 15 minutes until the mixture is smooth and elastic. It's allowed to be slightly tactile. Don't be tempted to add too much extra flour, as this will make it heavy. Wash the mixing bowl. Drizzle a little oil around the bowl and place the dough inside. Cover with cling film and then a clean dish towel. Leave in a warm place for 1–2 hours to prove. Alternatively you can leave it to prove in the fridge overnight.

Tip from the kitchen

We used to only eat pizza in Naples. Skills move – we now eat it anywhere south of Rome.

Preheat the oven to its highest setting.

This recipe makes enough dough for two 30cm square trays. Shape the dough into two equal-sized balls, rolling with your hands until smooth. Cover with a clean tea towel and leave to rest for a further 30–40 minutes.

We make this home-style pizza like Nonna Olivia used to make. Shallow baking trays work best. When the dough is ready, gently knock it down. If proving overnight, remove from the fridge half an hour before to allow it to come to temperature. Drizzle the tray with a little olive oil. Place the dough on top, stretching and squashing it to the edges to fill the space. Leave the dough, covered, to rest for another 20–30 minutes in a warm place.

Divide the salsa over the dough, spreading with the back of a spoon. Leave about 1–2cm clear at the edge.

Choose your toppings, as you wish, then drizzle with a little extra olive oil and bake for about 15 minutes until crisp.

PANDOLCE

Makes 2 loaves

10g fresh (5g dried) yeast

1 tsp sugar

475ml hand hot water

675g strong white flour

2 tsp salt

1 tsp ground cinnamon

½ tsp ground nutmeg

½ tsp ground mace

800g sultanas (or for a more aromatic flavour try 200g dried figs, chopped; 200g dried apricots, chopped; 200g dried cranberries or sour cherries, chopped; 200g walnuts, roughly chopped)

olive oil, to grease the bowl

butter, to grease the baking tray

1 egg, beaten, to glaze

This Tuscan bread is dense and packed with fruit. A fresh Pecorino or Gorgonzola Dolce, some figs (my favourite) and a little honey (delicious), and you could leave me to eat this all month and I'd be very happy.

Mix the yeast, sugar and water in a glass bowl and leave in a warm spot in the kitchen for about 15 minutes to allow the yeast to activate.

In a large bowl, mix the flour, salt and spices. Warm the bowl in the oven for a few minutes to heat the flour. Add the yeast mixture to the flour and combine well. If you are using an electric mixer, use the dough hook to beat until smooth. This will take about 10 minutes.

Fold in the fruit by hand, as you don't want it to be squashed. Transfer to a floured surface and knead until smooth and elastic. Add a little more flour, if required.

Rinse the mixing bowl and grease with a little oil. Place the dough in the bowl, cover with cling film and a clean, dry tea towel, and leave in a warm, draught-free part of the kitchen to double in size. This will take about 45 minutes.

Remove the dough from the bowl and place it on a floured surface. Knead very gently for another few minutes until the elasticity comes back. Divide the dough into two equal parts and shape each into a loaf. Place the dough on an oiled baking tray that will allow the dough to double in size. Cover with a damp cloth. Leave for another 30 minutes to 1 hour to allow the bread to rise again. Brush the bread with beaten egg. Bake in the middle of the oven at 230°C/450°F/Gas 8 for 20–25 minutes.

The bread will be well risen. When you turn it out of the tin, tap the bottom and the noise should sound hollow. Transfer to a wire rack and allow to cool. Enjoy while fresh, or after a day. This bread is traditionally sliced super thinly and toasted.

Tip from the kitchen

If you wake up every day with the same problem, it's time to talk to someone and get some help. Others can sometimes see the solution because they've not been staring at the problem.

BOMBOLONE

Makes 20

150g whole milk

55g caster sugar

10g fresh yeast

275g plain flour

¼ tsp salt

1 free-range egg

50g melted butter

oil for deep frying (a 20cm pot will hold about 1.5–2 litres of oil)

The first time I visited Rome was in 1983. When you go to an all-girls convent, school trips tend to be to holy places, but none of us complained about this one. Our highlight was the doughnuts the size of your head that were sold from kiosks in St Peter's Square. Light, delicious and dusted in sugar, I think they were 1,000 lira, my daily pocket money. The sugar stuck to my suncreamed cheeks in the blazing July heat. Licking your lips wasn't so good.

―――

Warm the milk, but don't let it boil. Add the sugar and yeast. Leave covered for about 20 minutes until it starts to froth. Sieve the flour and salt into a large warm mixing bowl and add the yeast mixture. Fold in the egg and butter. Mix with your electric dough hook until smooth with no lumps. Cover with cling film and allow to rest in the fridge for at least 4 hours or overnight.

Remove from the fridge and roll them by hand until smooth into golf ball-size shapes. Place on a sheet of greaseproof paper. Leave to rest for about 2 hours at room temperature before you start frying.

Choose a deep cast-iron casserole. Gather a slotted spoon for frying and a flat baking tray lined with a sheet of greaseproof paper. Heat the oil until it reaches 188°C/370°F.

Fry in small batches, turning regularly. The trick is to keep the oil at a constant temperature, so you need to add enough dough to help the others to cook and not burn. Each ball will take about 4 minutes. Remove when they are golden and the centre is fluffy and not pasty. Place on greaseproof paper to cool and drain any excess oil.

A dusting of caster sugar is essential for a good doughnut. A Kilner jar with a whole vanilla pod in the caster sugar adds a lovely extra layer of flavour to the sugar.

Zeppole

The further south in Italy you go, the more indulgent the doughnuts get. When you get to Naples, a custard filling turns the humble bombolone to a zeppole.

Add the cornflour to the caster sugar and the egg yolks and beat with a whisk. Heat the milk with the vanilla pod until it starts to steam, but not boil. Take it off the heat and add the hot milk to the egg mixture. Return to the heat and warm gently until it starts to thicken. Be very careful – it can curdle if it gets too hot. Use a whisk or wooden spoon to beat the mixture throughout the process, so it doesn't burn.

Remove from the heat and strain through a sieve, cover with greaseproof paper and allow to cool. Transfer to the fridge for at least 4 hours to set.

The crema pasticcera can be flavoured in a variety of different ways. It's thick so can hold these extra flavours. Use the above recipe as a base, and while still hot you can add any of the following:

Crema al pistacchio

Add 1 tablespoon of pistachio puree to the crema pasticcera. Dust the zeppoli in very finely ground toasted pistachios mixed with an equal quantity of vanilla-infused caster sugar.

Crema al limone

Add 1 tablespoon of limoncello to the crema pasticcera, with the zest of one unwaxed lemon.

Crema allo Strega

Add 1 tablespoon of Strega to the crema pasticcera. (Strega is the quintessential flavour for any Italian wedding, christening or birthday cake. One tablespoon may not be enough. For a liquor called 'witch' (the English translation of *strega*), it certainly cast a spell on me!)

Crema cioccolato

Add 100g of melted quality chocolate (70% cocoa) to the crema pasticcera.

For the Crema pasticcera

If you are confident, you can make this recipe without the cornflour. The cornflour just helps thicken the custard faster.

30g cornflour

70g caster sugar

5 free-range egg yolks

550ml whole milk

1 vanilla pod, cut in half to release the seeds

Tip from the kitchen

For an alternative Italian birthday cake, make the Genovese sponge (p. 192), make one batch of crema pasticcera, as above, then cut the sponge in half and drizzle generously with Strega. Lightly whip half a litre of double cream and fold it into the crema pasticcera. Place on top of the sponge. Place the remaining sponge over the cream mixture. Very lightly whip more double cream, about 1 litre. Lightly cover the cake with the cream – that magic palette knife will do the trick. If you're feeling fancy and you have an abundance of time on your hands, the cake would be topped with choux buns filled with chocolate crema pasticcera and a drizzle of simple white water icing. Some shaved chocolate on top will cover a multitude of sins. Refrigerate for about 2 hours, so it's easier to cut.

BIGNÈ AL CIOCCOLATO E CILIEGIE

Serves 4

For the pastry

75g strong white flour

pinch of salt

55g unsalted butter

120ml cold water

2 large eggs, lightly beaten

300ml double cream at room temperature

1 vanilla pod, seeds removed

For the chocolate sauce

200g bitter chocolate

100ml full fat milk

8 tbsp double cream

50g caster sugar

100g unsalted butter

100g quality preserved cherries in syrup, drained (Luxardo Maraschino are excellent)

Bignè (profiteroles) appear in every hotel dessert buffet and in most pasticceria cabinets. They are usually filled with a flavoured cream: vanilla, custard, lemon or coffee. The most indulgent are the chocolate varieties. In a restaurant, these are served with a warm chocolate sauce, always poured at the table, just to make you feel extra guilty.

Cut a large sheet of greaseproof paper about A3 size and sieve the flour and salt onto the paper.

Melt the butter in a saucepan with the water until it starts to heat – don't let it boil. Remove from the heat. Add the flour and beat with a wooden spoon until it forms a stiff ball. Transfer this to a large bowl and using an electric mixer slowly add the eggs. The mixture will be stiff.

Spoon golf ball-size balls of the dough onto a baking sheet lined with greaseproof paper. Splash the paper with a little cold water and then bake at 230°C/450°F/Gas 8 for 10 minutes, then 180°C/350°F/Gas 4 for 12–15 minutes until golden.

Remove from the oven and prick each bun with a toothpick to help the steam escape. This way, when the buns cool, they won't go soggy. Transfer to a wire rack.

Whip the double cream with the vanilla seeds – you can add a teaspoon of the syrup from the preserved cherries for a little extra colour, if you like. When the buns are cold, fill them with the cream. Do not store in the fridge.

To make the chocolate sauce, break the chocolate into small pieces and place in a glass bowl. Bring the milk to the boil and pour over the chocolate. Mix until smooth.

In a small saucepan, melt the cream, sugar and butter until all dissolved. Add the melted chocolate mixture and beat until silky. Fold in the cherries and serve seductively over the bignè.

BISCOTTI AL PECORINO

Makes about 70

200g unsalted butter

zest of 1 unwaxed Amalfi lemon

300g plain flour

75g cornflour

1 tsp sea salt flakes

200g Pecorino Romano, finely grated

2 sprigs fresh thyme

If ever there was a hint to our Italian Scottish roots, it has to be this. Pecorino shortbread. Delicious to enjoy as a homemade salty aperitivo nibble.

———

Preheat the oven to 180°C/350°F/Gas 4 and line a baking sheet with parchment paper.

Cream the butter until light and fluffy, and add the lemon zest. Slowly beat in the flour, cornflour and salt until well incorporated. Finally beat in the grated pecorino and the thyme leaves. Transfer to a floured surface and knead until bound together. It's very crumbly, don't worry.

Form into a rolling-pin shape, wrap in cling film and refrigerate. Remove from the fridge and cut into 5mm slices. Place on a parchment-lined baking sheet. Bake in the preheated oven for about 8–10 minutes until golden. Transfer to a wire rack to cool.

Tip from the kitchen

Be happy. It's sometimes easier than you think.

MANDORLE

Makes 1 family batch

4 free-range egg whites

300g icing sugar

zest of 1 unwaxed orange

35ml orange juice

½ tsp orange blossom water

500g blanched almonds, very lightly toasted and, when cool, ground in a food processor

Most mornings I head to Contini George Street to start the day. I hang up my coat, wash my hands, open my laptop and by the time I sit down my water glass has been filled and a cappuccino has arrived, with one of these delicious super soft almond biscuits dangling off the side of the saucer, tempting me to eat it. I love our team.

Prepare a flat baking sheet and line with greaseproof paper. Heat the oven to 160°C/325°F/Gas 3.

Lightly beat the egg whites in a mixer and add the icing sugar, orange zest and juice, and orange blossom water. You aren't making meringues, so the mixture should be just combined, not beaten to a soft peak texture. Gently fold in the ground almonds to make a paste.

Roll the mixture into walnut-sized balls and place on the tray, pressing down ever so slightly so their bottoms spread onto the paper. Bake for 10–15 minutes until golden. Allow to cool and dust with a little extra icing sugar to finish.

These store for up to a week in an airtight container.

Tip from the kitchen

As an alternative to the orange flavours, substitute the zest and orange blossom water with 35ml Amaretto liqueur. Top each biscuit with a whole almond before you bake. Two biscuits in one recipe. For a third recipe, substitute the almonds for pistachios and swap the orange blossom and orange zest for lemon zest and 1 teaspoon of vanilla extract. As usual, a good foundation allows you to build many different structures.

FINOCCHIO

6 cups plain flour

1 cup caster sugar

6 tsp fennel seeds

1 cup extra virgin olive oil

1 large free-range egg

1 cup white wine

finely grated zest of ½ lemon

1 tsp vanilla extract

1 egg, to glaze

extra caster sugar, to sprinkle on top

These are traditional biscuits from our village. No visit from an aunty was complete without a bag of these beauties. This is Zia Pierina's recipe (Victor's aunt).

Makes enough for No. 1 son. Let's face it, the boys were always the favourites . . .

Choose a large mixing bowl and add the dry ingredients. Next add the oil, egg, white wine, lemon zest and vanilla, and mix well. You can do this with a wooden spoon, or by hand works even better.

Choose two flat baking sheets and line them with greaseproof paper. Take a walnut-size ball of the mixture and roll with a little extra flour into a sausage shape, then stick the ends together to form a misshapen circle. Place this on the baking sheet and continue until all the mixture is used up.

Brush with a little of the egg wash and sprinkle with a pinch of caster sugar. Bake at 180°C/350°F/Gas 4 for 20 minutes until golden. Remove from the oven and allow to cool on a wire rack. You want the biscuits to have a crunch; they shouldn't be soft.

Tip from the kitchen

These biscuits are perfect for a cup of tea or for dipping in a dessert wine, such as a Vin Santo. They keep for up to a week in a sealed container, but never last for more than a day in our house.

TORTA DI RICOTTA

Serves 6

For the pastry

250g self-raising flour, plus extra for dusting

pinch of salt

125g unsalted butter, chilled

100g caster sugar

1 egg yolk

1 tbsp ice-cold water

1 tbsp lemon juice

For the filling

700g ricotta

100g icing sugar

3 large free-range eggs

zest of 1 unwaxed orange

50g fresh candied orange peel

50g quality chocolate chips (70% cocoa)

If you're on holiday in Italy and staying in a hotel – either a big posh one or a little family-run one – the chances are the loveliest cook in the kitchen, or the next door bakery (I'm saying this because you have to be lovely to want to bake for breakfast), will have made you this sweet, heavenly tart. I think of it as the Italian substitute for a morning croissant or freshly baked scone. It's not too sweet, just lovely sweet, like the cooks.

First, make the pastry. Sieve the flour and salt into a large mixing bowl and coarsely grate the butter on top. Dip the butter into the flour to stop it sticking to the grater. Rub the butter into the flour using your fingertips until it resembles coarse breadcrumbs. Add the sugar and mix through, then add the egg yolk and bind with the water and lemon juice until the mixture forms a ball. Place on a floured surface and knead gently. Transfer to a bowl and refrigerate for about 30 minutes.

To make the filling, sieve the ricotta into a bowl and then beat in the icing sugar and the eggs with a wooden spoon until the mixture is smooth. Fold in the zest, peel and chocolate chips.

Remove the pastry from the fridge and let it come to room temperature. On a floured surface roll it out and line a well-buttered 25cm loose-bottom flan tin. Freeze the lined pastry tin for about 30 minutes. This helps stop the pastry shrinking when it's cooking.

Warning: I like a soggy cake bottom, so I leave it up to you to decide if you want to blind bake the pastry or not.

Fill the pastry tin with the ricotta mixture and bake at 180°C/350°F/Gas 4 for 30–40 minutes until light and golden. Allow to cool and enjoy for the next few mornings with a cup of milky coffee. Feel like you're on holiday in Italy with a lovely cook in the kitchen.

Tip from the kitchen

Say a prayer when you bake a cake. Saint Zita was the patron saint of little cooks. Her bread was never burnt when she stayed too long in church. I can't guarantee an angel will remove your baking from the oven, but somehow a moment's contemplation reminds you to set a timer.

PIEMONTE & LIGURIA

One of my earliest memories of drinking alcohol is wine served from a Chianti flask, the wicker binding now so synonymous with Italian red wine. It is believed to have been introduced by the glass blowers of the Arno (the river that runs through Tuscany) either as an excellent marketing tool or simply to protect the bottles and stop them clanking together and breaking. A photo of my grandfather in 1914 holding a bottle of local wine from Lazio clearly shows the tradition was adopted in many other parts of Italy.

While Chianti may be the most widely known and drunk Italian red wine, Piemonte holds the title for the aficionados' favourites, from Barolo to Barbaresco, some of the most expensive in the world. At the other end of the scale, the sweet sparkling Moscato from Asti, another Piemonte town, is my favourite celebration sweet dessert wine. Birthday cake and chilled Fontanafredda are good reasons to be a year older.

Victor is my wingman and my wine man. I'm not adventurous with alcohol. I always go back to the drinks I know I like. Our travels around the regions of Italy have, to some degree, been the same. Piemonte is an adventure I am yet to have, other than passing though Malpensa, one of north Italy's airports, which serves Milan and the Alps.

Bra is the centre of Slow Food, a movement we've championed for years. Founded by Carlo Petrini almost 40 years ago, as a challenge to the global food system, it is now represented in every continent around the world, with millions of members.

Piemonte is as rich a region of Italy as any.

Bordering France in part, it's not somewhere you immediately think of as Italian – maybe why it's sometimes called Piedmont, rather than its Italian name, Piemonte.

Some of its towns hold the crowns for the world's best. The heart of the Kingdom of Savoy, the engine room for the unification of Italy, and in its early days its capital. The Royal Residencies built around the seventeenth and eighteenth centuries are definitely worth a trip, so much so they are on the UNESCO listing. Alba, a favourite haunt of Victor's when travelling without me, is most famous for its truffles. The white variety sometimes sells for more than £30,000 per kilo. It's more uncommonly known as the home of Ferrero Rocher – I don't get the fuss over these chocolates; the bits always get stuck in my teeth.

Barolo is known for its red wines, the producer Gaja having the reputation for the most expensive wines in the world in the 1980s and

1990s. Lago Maggiore, the largest of the Italian lakes, falls within this region.

Liguria is the Italian Riviera, with Genova as its capital. This is where Nonno Carlo was based as a mounted policeman before he moved to Scotland. All the really glamorous spots sit on this coast: Cinque Terre, Santa Margherita and Portofino. Neighbouring the border of Monaco, it's not hard to see where it gets its reputation. This is the home of la dolce vita.

I've lived a lifetime in Scotland and there are still dozens of towns here I've not had the time to visit, or to visit often enough to know well. In Italy, it is no different. There is so much to celebrate. Victor and I still have so very much to learn and see in Italy, but we feel so blessed to have this country as part of our heritage. We feel blessed to have Scotland as our home. Our grandparents got it right – despite the weather. We thank them for bringing us here but leaving those strings that connect us back to their roots. Who knows what decisions our children will make. We've definitely had the best of both worlds.

BACI

Makes a 350g gift box

200ml double cream, measured into 2 x 100ml amounts

100g hazelnuts, roasted and skins removed, then roughly chopped

225g Valrhona dark chocolate (55% cocoa)

premium quality cocoa powder, for dusting

Expensive chocolates make me think of my parents returning from holiday. They never took us with them. We never complained and we never complained about the fancy chocolates or new exotic food we got when they came home.

Combining the flavours of chocolate and hazelnuts that I associate with Piemonte are the pretty but mass-produced Baci from Perugia in Umbria. These blue-wrapped morsels come with a love note, which makes up for the chocolate.

Put 100ml of cream and the hazelnuts in a pan over a low heat. Remove from the heat when the cream begins to steam, but before it boils. Leave to cool for 10 minutes and then blend in a food processor until smooth. Sieve through a fine sieve and set aside.

Meanwhile, chop, grate or break up the chocolate into very small pieces and place in a heatproof glass bowl over a bain-marie. Do not let the simmering water touch the bottom of the bowl.

Strain the remaining cream into a clean pan and put it over a low heat but, again, do not let it boil.

When the cream is hot, pour it over the chocolate. Stir slowly until the chocolate has melted and then add the hazelnut cream.

Pour the mixture into a 20cm silicone mould and place in the fridge to allow it to set for 30 mins. Remove from the fridge.

Dust a board with cocoa powder as if you are flouring a surface to roll out pastry. Gently turn the chocolate onto the dusted surface and remove the silicone. Dust the top of the chocolate with more cocoa. Using a hot knife that has been dipped in boiling water and dried, cut the block into small squares, no more than 1.5cm square, and roll into a ball. Dust each square in more cocoa and place on a plate or in a gift box lined with baking parchment. Best enjoyed within 3 days of making. Store in the fridge.

Remove from the fridge before you serve them.

Tip from the kitchen

Don't be too proud to say sorry. Kiss and make up. You might be rewarded with chocolates, who knows? Un bacio x

Bevande

FRAGOLA FRA

Serves 6

300g fresh strawberries, stalks removed

squeeze of fresh lemon juice

1 tbsp agave syrup (enough to your taste, depending on the sweetness of the fruit)

1 bottle of prosecco, super chilled

6 strawberries, to decorate the glasses

6 sprigs of fresh mint, for decoration

Growing up as one of eight children never felt normal. Being the only Italians and Catholics in a tiny Scottish village was another challenge. My father was always adamant that we only spoke English. The Italian classes at school had no effect – my Italian, except my food Italian, is grammatically shocking. We ate Italian and we listened to Italian music. None of my family are at all musical. We do struggle to find a collective skill other than a love of food. One of my favourite songs, sung by an uncle or some distant relative at Christmas, was 'Fravula Fra', famously sung by Roberto Murolo, and this delicious aperitivo reminds me of it.

Blend the strawberries and lemon juice with the agave in a food processor. Sieve to remove any pips and chill for at least 1 hour until the mixture is cold.

Choose a chilled rocks glass and divide this mixture between six glasses, add a few ice cubes and top with prosecco.

Decorate with a strawberry, a sprig of mint and a straw.

For a non-alcoholic version, swap the prosecco for chilled San Pellegrino mineral water and lots of ice. This is a particularly fizzy water, so it's very good as a mixer. Add a large slice of lemon.

Tip from the kitchen

No phones at the dinner table. We have had as many 'animated discussions' as we've had laughs at our dinner table. Passions run deep. Our children have challenged our views more than we have ever challenged ourselves. We thank them so very much for broadening our minds and helping us see the world from a different perspective, mostly from the dining table.

NOTTE NOCINO

50ml hazelnut milk

25ml Frangelico

25ml Amaro Nonino

25ml vodka

freshly grated nutmeg, to finish

Nut milks have been popular in Italy for ever. I love almond milk chilled in the fridge to almost frozen with a squeeze of fresh lemon juice. No. 1 big brother introduced this to me years ago. It's so refreshing when it's hot, hot, hot.

When it's colder, hazelnut milk can give a more cosy comfort. The classic Brandy Alexander is a very sophisticated after-dinner drink. I find it very alcoholic and it's not very Italian. This inspired version will get you *parlare Italiano*.

Fill a cocktail shaker with ice and add all the ingredients, except the nutmeg. Shake for 20 seconds and then drain into a chilled martini glass. Finish with a grating of nutmeg.

Tip from the kitchen

Practise what I preach. Do as I say, not as I do. I never learn.

NEGRONI

Camparino Negroni

25ml Bulldog Gin (we use Bombay Sapphire Premier Cru)

25ml Campari (of course)

25ml 1757 Vermouth di Torino Rosso

twist of orange peel, to decorate

Negroni Sbagliato

25ml Campari

25ml Martini Rosso

50ml Prosecco

Believed to have been invented in Caffè Casoni in Florence in 1919 – clearly a good year (it was the year of my father's birth too).

The Americano is made with Campari, vermouth and topped with soda. The story goes that Count Camillo Negroni wanted something with a little more punch, so he substituted the soda for gin. This Italian classic is everything a cocktail should be: elegant, sophisticated, good to look at and intoxicating. Victor and my children love a Negroni. I like the lighter version, a Sbagliato, the version without the gin but topped with Prosecco.

There are so many great gins to choose from – Victor's favourite is Isle of Harris – but for a Negroni he loves Cannonball Gin, named after Cannonball House, where we have our restaurant. It's 57.2% ABV, so definitely for the heavyweights.

Camparino Negroni

The ultimate Negroni is the Camparino Negroni. One of the world's best bars, the Camparino is situated in the Galleria in Piazza del Duomo in Milan. The bar is owned by the family who own Campari and Aperol. This is their version.

Fill a tall glass cocktail shaker with ice and add each measure. Very gently stir the liquid around the ice. They say this should take a minimum of 5 minutes. This allows the ice to cool the spirits gently and it also allows a little of the water from the ice to help infuse all the flavours.

Serve strained in a rocks glass with more ice and a twist of orange.

Negroni Sbagliato

This is for me – my favourite aperitivo. Nothing else to say.

Served over ice with an orange twist.

Tip from the kitchen

Everything in moderation – apart from cuddles from those you love.

ANGURIA

50ml Grey Goose vodka

25ml Campari

50g fresh watermelon puree

2–3 drops basil essence

1 egg white

2–3 drops plum bitter

My other go-to drink is a Campari fresh orange. Upgrade to freshly squeezed Tarocco oranges and, as Tina Turner would say, it's 'simply the best'. This combination with fresh watermelon is pretty close.

———

Pour all the ingredients into a shaker, dry shake gently, and ice and shake again. Pour into a glass over ice with a single strain, and garnish and serve with a straw.

POMPELMO

100ml freshly pressed pink grapefruit juice

1 x bottle San Bitter

splash of soda

slice of grapefruit

ice

A non-alcoholic interpretation of the above.

———

Choose a high ball and fill with ice. Add the grapefruit juice, and top up with San Bitter and a splash of soda. Serve with a slice of grapefruit.

Tip from the kitchen
———
Each stage of life is a gift. I'm just past the middle, hopefully. It's interesting watching how the older and younger generations can still learn from each other.

SPRITZ

25ml Aperol (or other choice)

100ml prosecco

4–5 ice cubes

slice of orange, or my favourite and definitely more classic, a large Sicilian Nocellara olive (this transforms the drink to Milano, halfway between Sicily and Scotland)

splash of sparkling mineral water, to serve

No. 1 son attended his first wedding in Italy when he was seventeen and discovered the classic Aperol Spritz. He says it was his favourite wedding. When we first opened on George Street in 2004, we called this iconic Milanese drink a George Street Irn Bru. I'm convinced the founder of Barr's travelled to Milan and partook in the afternoon ritual of drinks and snacking after work, enjoying an Aperol Spritz, and came back and invented Scotland's national drink. Ginseng and rhubarb form the basis of the Italian version; the Scottish one looks and smells almost the same, it just doesn't have the alcohol. Perhaps why No. 1 son enjoyed the wedding so much . . .

This basic recipe works for a whole range of spritz, so if you're in the mood for a change why not try substituting the Aperol, which is by far the sweetest of these other bitters combinations.

Campari – if you want to be a little more sophisticated, this is the alternative. Serve with a slice of pink grapefruit.

Cynar – if you want to be a little more interesting, it's made from artichokes. Lovely with a large Cerignola olive on a stick.

Punt e Mes – if you want to confuse everyone . . .

Cinzano Bianco – if you want to go all out '70s, with the alternative sweet version to Aperol. Serve with two straws – it's so sweet, you'll think you're drinking lemonade.

L'Aperitivo Nonino – in 2020 this won an award for 'the best aperitivo in the world'. We wouldn't expect anything else from this distinguished distilling family. Serve with a slice of lemon.

Limoncello – a new take on a spritz, it's zingy and delicious. Serve with a slice of Amalfi lemon, naturally.

Aperol – if you like Irn Bru . . .

Tip from the kitchen

Surround yourself with people you love. It's equally important to make sure these people love you back.

VIN BRULÉ

750ml red wine, such as a light Bardolino

50g golden caster sugar

1 unwaxed orange, studded with 8 cloves, then cut into quarters

1 unwaxed lemon, studded with 8 cloves, then cut into quarters

1 stick of cinnamon

3 star anise

Something like mulled wine seems so simple that I maybe don't need to include it, but it is one of my favourite things. I make it every year when the children dress the Christmas tree (before I redress it once everyone else has gone to bed) and I start writing Christmas cards. The years have passed and the children are young adults now, and better at home decorating than me. After a few glasses of this, trust me, I'm in no state to be dressing anything.

Place all the ingredients into a pot and gently simmer for 20 minutes to allow the flavours to release. Serve in small glasses.

Tip from the kitchen

If you spill red wine on the carpet, don't waste white wine to clean it up. Get the Cif out instead.

ESPRESSO MARTINI

50ml vodka (wheat-based vodka is my preference)

25ml Kahlúa

single shot of espresso

15ml gomme syrup

3 coffee beans to garnish

I've included this, as it really is one of the drinks of this generation, and very popular as an after-dinner cocktail at Contini George Street.

Chill a martini glass.

Add the ingredients to a Boston shaker filled with ice, saving the coffee beans for decoration. Shake for 20 seconds and strain into the chilled glass.

Arrange the coffee beans on top.

Tip from the kitchen

Don't take your health for granted. Don't take your family for granted. Don't take your friends for granted. Don't take the beautiful world around us for granted.

VINI

I am no wine expert. Thankfully, Victor loves wine, especially *Italian* wine – any other country and we're both totally out of our territory. Here are Victor's Italian wine cellar notes, where he shares some of his favourite grape varieties and favourite wines.

We all have a different palate and different preferences; there is no right taste for everyone. Nonna G stopped drinking red wine or anything with bubbles when she turned 92. As long as it was white, she liked it – a bit like her outfits. I like low alcohol wines, so anything over 13% and it generally goes straight to my head. Younger wines tend to be more to my taste, but when you get to indulge in some of the really, really good – even great – older wines, it's not hard to see why they are enjoyed and celebrated as much as they are. Victor loves the old classics and gets excited about the unusual.

If nothing else, I hope this may add a little wider understanding of the complexities of Italian wine. With more than 2,000 indigenous grape varieties, it's a warehouse full.

We do love a glass of sparkling wine or a cocktail as an aperitivo. Enjoying a different wine with different foods is a given. Yes, for special occasions we do like a little white, a little red and a little dessert matched to each course. Midweek, one glass of wine will serve us very well.

In the restaurants, we've always offered a range of wines by the glass. Restaurants should give you the opportunity to try flavours you might not be tempted to at home. Please always ask our team to taste a wine you're curious about; we'll share with pleasure. Enjoying different wines by the glass with each course can also be more fun than sharing a whole bottle one of you may not like. It usually means you drink less too, which may or may not be the objective.

Classifications of wine

Italy loves a little regulation. Well, *a lot* of regulation. Here are some of the key classifications that are used when making and bottling wine.

DOC (Denominazione di Origine Controllata): There are over 330 DOCs in Italy, each with their own rules, guaranteeing quality based on geographical area. These wines are assessed by an approved panel before release. Montepulciano d'Abruzzo DOC is an example.

DOCG (Denominazione di Origine Controllata e Garantita): This is the highest classification of Italian wines. Each part of the production process is carefully regulated, from the transportation of grapes to the work in the cellar, to how (and when) wines are bottled. Grapes must be sourced from a specific geographical area and the wines are assessed by two expert panels before release. For example, our beautiful Bellavista sparkling wine is from Franciacorta DOCG.

IGT (Indicazione Geografica Tipica): This classification indicates a quality wine made in a particular geographic area which doesn't adhere to the rules of a DOC or DOCG. For example, 'Super Tuscan' wines don't meet the rules of DOC or DOCG wines, as they blend Bordeaux varieties (e.g. Cabernet Sauvignon or Merlot) with Sangiovese, yet they are still made in Tuscany to a high standard. As a result, these wines are labelled IGT Toscana. Tenuta San Guido 'Sassicaia' or Antinori 'Tignanello' are great examples.

VdT (Vino da Tavola): Describes an Italian table wine made using grapes grown anywhere in the country. They are of reasonable quality that is best drunk with a meal. My kind of wine.

Varieties of Grape

What is sometimes difficult to understand is the wine may not be the grape variety. Chianti, for example, is not a grape. Sangiovese is the grape from the region of Chianti. Hopefully the following will help with the basics.

Personal taste does come into play, but care and quality of the growing and production process is reflected in the final price for almost everything in life. Wine is no exception.

White grape varieties

Arnies: translated as 'little rascal', it has a Piemonte pedigree. It is clean, crisp and very good with deep-fried foods.

Falanghina: an ancient grape variety believed to be of Greek origin. It's beautiful with shellfish.

Fiano: a delicious, extremely quaffable, quality grape, largely grown in Campania. It's particularly well matched to fish and seafood.

Gewurztraminer: this has always been one of Victor's favourite grapes. Higher in alcohol, full bodied and best described as chunky and rich.

Malvasia: an ancient grape variety that's often sweet and dry. It's unusual and worth trying if you are looking for something different. It will match well with light tomato dishes.

Maturano: the indigenous grape variety from our region and used by my brother to make his very unusual, delicious and distinctive Matrimonio and Nostalgia wines.

Pecorino: this has its home in the Marche and Abruzzo regions. Slightly floral, and matches beautifully with roast lamb, veal or, my favourite, goat.

Pinot bianco: can be referred to, by non-Italians, as Chardonnay's understudy. When unoaked, I love it. Perfect for creamy dishes or risotto.

Pinot grigio: one of the most popular grapes in the world, probably because it's so charming and easy to drink. A great all-rounder.

Trebbiano: one of the most prolific Italian white grape varieties. An all-round reliable light wine.

Verdicchio: usually grown in the Marche region. It has a rich, buttery, almost almond flavour, which makes it a great match for cured meats.

Vermentino: mostly from Liguria and Sardinia. Similar in style to Sauvignon blanc. It will match particularly well with distinctive, slightly bitter flavours like artichokes and courgettes.

Red grape varieties

Aglianico: an elusive southern varietal. The best are grown on volcanic soils. Worth trying, if you spot it.

Barbera: another grape largely grown in Piemonte. Matches well to mushrooms, blue cheese and bitter green vegetables.

Cesanese: an ancient Roman variety and one of Victor's all-time favourites. It will always sit happily beside a plate of carbonara or amatriciana.

Corvina: an indigenous grape from Veneto. Light, fresh and easy-drinking red.

Dolcetto: another Piemonte baby. Rich, but soft and cuddly. Classy, complex and medium-bodied.

Montepulciano: from Abruzzo, this grape will never fail alongside any rich ragù, anchovy flavour or oily bruschetta.

Nebbiolo: the grape of Piemonte. Always perfectly partnered with those iconic fresh truffles from the region.

Negroamaro: a Puglian star that is fruity and full of flavour.

Nero d'Avola: the classic Sicilian grape. You can taste all that sunshine in this full-bodied, fruity grape.

Pinot nero: grows most happily in the Alto Adige. It's usually lighter, and will marry beautifully with grilled meat, and always with freshly cracked chunks of young pecorino.

Primitivo: a robust and enthusiastic Puglian grape that has supported many northern Italian wineries for years, without anyone noticing or knowing.

Sangiovese: one of Italy's most Italian red grape varieties. It will never let you down.

Some styles of Italian wines

These wines can be made from one or multiple grape varieties, depending on the DOC/DOCG rules governing their production. I've listed them to give a little extra knowledge and understanding around not only the grapes themselves but the wines that we often end up enjoying the most.

Amarone and its slightly fruitier best friend, *Valpolicella*: both are made in Veneto from Corvina and Rondinella grapes. Valpolicella is made without ageing, while Amarone is made by fermenting dried grapes and ageing them for two years. These are big flavours that your palate needs time to learn to appreciate. Look out for Valpolicella Ripasso if you like that richer Amarone style but without the price tag. A pastime worth investing in?

Barbaresco: another Piemonte bottled perfection made from 100 per cent Nebbiolo. It is usually slightly lighter than its big brother, Barolo. Far more to my taste. I'll leave the Barolo to Victor.

Bardolino: made with Corvina, Rondinella and Molinara grapes with up to 15 per cent of a selection of another four grape varieties in any combination. From an area around Lake Garda, Bardolino is as fresh as the air around the surrounding mountains.

Barolo: made from Nebbiolo grapes, you feel the luxury of this premium Piemonte wine. Its earthy tones work brilliantly with that other regional treasure, truffles.

Brunello: a Tuscan king of wines. It's made from Brunello grapes, which are Sangiovese grapes but from this very small town surrounding Montalcino, proving yet again that terroir alone creates very different final flavours and prices to match.

Chianti: what could be more Italian than this masterpiece? Made from Sangiovese grapes, it's a champion.

Franciacorta: Sparkling wine from Lombardy, made in the traditional method (or 'Metodo Classico') also used for Champagne, Cava and English sparkling wine. Made from Chardonnay, Pinot nero and Pinot bianco, it is often called the champagne of Italy. We stock Bellavista, the wine we chose for our wedding.

Gavi: from Piemonte. Always one of our most popular wines, made from Cortese. Crisp, clean and so drinkable. No wonder it's regarded as one of Italy's best.

Lambrusco: an example of the DOC also being the name of the grape. Lambrusco is used to make the red sparkling wine from Emilia-Romagna. It can be sweet, but the classy version is dry. Best served chilled. Yes, fizzy red wine served chilled – it's not a cliché, it's clever.

Lugana: another winner from the shores of Lake Garda, this is made from Turbiana grapes. Elegant, clean and robust enough to be enjoyed by both of us.

Orvieto: made from a blend of Grechetto, Trebbiano and Verdelho grapes from Umbria. This wine used to be slightly sweeter – my father, as he got older, always chose this – now, it tends to be lighter and dryer. Very delicious with fish.

Prosecco: the famous sparkling wine from Veneto. Made using the Charmat method and produced from Glera, originally called Prosecco Tondo. A perfect aperitivo. There are many proseccos but some of the best are the DOC regulated from the Valdobbiadene and notably Cartizze.

Soave: from Veneto, this is an incredibly elegant, light white wine with hints of peaches and melon, made from Garganica grapes.

Vin Santo or Holy Wine: a uniquely Tuscan farmers' tradition, taken as a welcome drink – their equivalent to our cup of tea. The Italians do have style. Fashion has allowed this to evolve into one of the world's most famous dessert wines. The grapes are hung indoors over the winter to naturally raisin, concentrating the sugars to create a sweet wine once fermented. It has a price to match the time and skill needed to produce it. Cantuccini (almond biscuits) are served alongside it. I'm sorry to say even the Italian rich tea biscuit is classier.

DIGESTIVI

An Italian meal is never finished until you've enjoyed an espresso. If it's been a very special meal, we have to add a digestivo. A corretto is an espresso with a dash of liquor – a little splash designed to aid digestion and (they say) improve your health. The second part may be true, only to rebalance and soothe the indulgences before.

Amaro: a bitter distillation of herbs. Usually around 28–30% ABV.

Amaro Averna: a Sicilian digestivo that has a sweeter herb flavour, from the very remote mountaintop village of Caltanissetta. (29% ABV)

Amaro Ciociaro: the digestivo of our region and always on Victor's drink shelf – or should I say, medicine cupboard. It's slightly different, as it's a distillation of herbs and wine. (30% ABV)

Amaro Lucano: the labels of these bottles are more beautiful than the contents. A secret recipe of more than 30 herbs from Basilicata, this is a very traditional, but loved, amaro. (28% ABV)

Amaro Nonino: the Nonino family version is the most elegant and smooth of any we've tasted, but at a surprising 35% ABV. Serve over ice with a generous slice of orange. It's a very civilised way to finish dinner. Alternatively, you can enjoy a shot with that heavenly coffee/gelato combination, an affogato. Sumptuous.

Anice Forte: star anise flavour, with a lower sugar but higher alcohol content than sambuca. It was always Nonna Olivia's corretto. Many afternoons were lost with much laughter and a bottle on the Brunswick Street kitchen table. (40% ABV)

Fernet Branca: my family served this on a spoon for medicinal reasons. It's brutal. We were given it from primary school age. Punishment or prevention? (39% ABV)

Frangelico: a 300-year-old recipe named after a monk has got to be good. I prefer this hazelnut flavour to the more commercially popular Amaretto, which is made from the distillation of apricot kernels, not almonds. (20% ABV)

Grappa Nonino: Grappa has an interesting reputation. Grape must (the by-product of winemaking) is distilled to a 40+% ABV that sometimes can be described as paint-stripper. Not Nonino. This fourth generation dynasty from Friuli developed the distillation of the grape as a primary product. With a range of over 40 distillates, there really is a grappa for every taste.

Limoncello Di Capri IGP: made on Capri, with fresh lemons from the island and neighbouring Sorrento. This IGP is the classy version of this popular distillation. Serve ice cold in a frozen shot glass for a shot of summer. (30% ABV)

Sambuca Molinari: you'll recognise this as the fun, flaming version with three coffee beans gently floating on that clear, viscous liquorice liquor. (40% ABV)

POSSO LASCIARE LA TAVOLA?
(Please can I leave the table?)

The most important loves of my life, this book is dedicated to you.

Victor, my best friend and darling husband.

After eight years of marriage, the babies finally started to arrive. We'd been told we couldn't have children. For anyone wanting a family, my heart goes out to them.

Orlando, our beautiful boy, No. 1 son

Carla, our sweetheart, No. 1 daughter

Arianna, our darling, No. 3 and we got it right

Rocco – our Cocker Spaniel, our little bundle of joy

Establishing a business when you have young children is a challenge. Carla was born in December and we opened at George Street in April. The following Christmas Day (the only day of the year we close) No. 3 arrived. With three babies under three, we had our hands full. At times it has felt impossible. The worst parts pass and thankfully the good parts have left much happier memories. I'm older, wiser and more grateful than ever.

Thank you to our team, our suppliers and our partners. There are many parts to hospitality and each is as important.

Thank you also to the team at Birlinn: Debs, in particular, for her patience in accepting all my edits. It's been a pleasure and a joy working with an established Edinburgh publishing house. We really are very lucky to live in Scotland.

A special thank you to Ambar D'Andrea, for her beautiful photography, working up to the day before her baby, Cameron, was born.

Alina, what more can I say? You're our favourite. Hands up who loves Alina!

I so very much hope you've enjoyed my stories and that these recipes become part of your kitchen. Enjoy cooking, and sharing good food and making happy memories with the people you love and love you back.

Keep well, keep safe, keep cooking and *buon appetito*.

The only thing left to do is the dishes. Victor can do the glasses.

Carina

INDEX

Aglianico (grape variety) 245
Alba, truffles, Piemonte 16, 116, 227
Alberobello, Puglia 147
almonds
    Mandorle 220
    Mandorle Speziate 50
    Marzipan 193
    Notte Nocino 233
    Torta di Fichi e Mandorle 189
Amalfi 111
Amalfi lemons (recipe) 176
    Apertivi 50
    Biscotti al Pecorino 219
    Melograno 176
Amaro Averna 248
Amaro Ciociaro 248
Amaro Lucano 248
Amaro Nonino 248
Amarone 246
Amatriciana (pasta) 94
Anguria (cocktail) 236
Anguria e Caprino (salad) 169
Anice Forte (digestivi) 248
Antiche Carampane, Venice 49
Aperitivi 50
    Contini Olives 50
    Mandorle Speziate 50
    Noci con Miele 50
Aperol Spritz 239
Aragosta (lobster) 119
Arancia (Orange) 172
    Crema di arancia 199
    Sciroppo di arancia e zafferano 191
Arancini 53
Arnies (grape variety) 244
Artichokes (Carciofi) 159
    Crudi 166
    Cynar 239
Asiago (cheese) 40, 48
Asparagi 155
aubergines
    Fritti 35
    Melanzane alla Parmigiana 152
    Verdure 151

baccalà (salt cod) 34
Baci 229
Barbaresco 246
Barbera (grape variety) 245
Bardolino 246
Barolo, Piemonte 227

Barolo (wine) 246
Battuto do lardo 65
béchamel 152
Bignè (profiteroles) al Cioccolato e Ciliegie 217
Biscotti al Pecorino 219
biscuits
    Biscotti al Pecorino 219
    Finocchio 223
    Mandorle 220
Boboli Gardens, Florence 71
Bollito Misto 136
Bologna 122–3
Bombolone 214–16
Bottura, Massimo 123
Branzino (Sea bass) 106
breads
    Bruschetta 45
    Focaccia 209
    Mozzarella in Carrozza 38
    Pandolce 213
    Panettone Pudding 199
    Panzanella (salad) 185
    Pizza al Taglio 210
Brenner Pass 201
Broccoletti (pasta) 83
Brodo (soup) 67
Brodo di Carne (soup) 68
Brunello (wine) 247
bruschetta 45–7
    al pistacchio 46
    al pomodoro 46
    all'aglio 46
    con crema di baccalà mantecato 47
Butter sugo 79
butters
    Burro al limone 101
    Burro al peperoncino 151
    Burro all'aglio 64
    Larder notes 25

Cacio e pepe 88
Caffè Florian, Venice 49
Calamari Fritti 103
Campania 110–11
Campari spritz 239
Camparino Negroni 235
Campo de' Fiori, Rome 86
cannellini beans
    Crema di Canellini 149
    Pasta e Fagioli 58

Cantine del Vino già Schiavi 49
Capesante (Scallops) 102
Carbonara 91
Carciofi (Artichokes) 159
    Crudi 166
    Cynar spritz 239
Carpaccio di Pesce 37
Cassata 192–3
Cavolfiore (Cauliflower) 181
Ceci e Patate (soup) 73
Cesanese (grape variety) 245
Chianti 247
chicken
    Bollito Misto 136
    Brodo 67
    Coniglio all'Ischitana 131
    Milanese 132
    Pollo 139
    stock 67
cicchetti 49
Cinzano Bianco spritz 239
Ciociaria 28–9
classifications
    of food 22
    of vini 243–4
Coniglio all'Ischitana 131
Contadino (pasta) 92
Contini, Carina 1, 9–13, 48, 170–1
Contini Olives 50
Corvina (grape variety) 245
Cozze (Mussels) 113
Crema di arancia 199
Crema di baccalà mantecato (dip) 47
Crema di Cannellini (dip) 149
Crema di Funghi (soup) 64
Crema di Patate (potatoes) 129
Crema di Pomodoro (soup) 63
crema pasticcera 216
    al limone 216
    al pistacchio 216
    allo Strega 216
    cioccolato 216
Crudi 166
Cynar spritz 239

Da Raffaele, trattoria 111
Digestivi 248–9
    Amaro Averna 248
    Amaro Ciociaro 248
    Amaro Lucano 248
    Amaro Nonino 248
    Anice Forte 248
    Fernet Branca 249
    Frangelico 249
    Grappa Nonino 248
    Limoncello Di Capri IGP 249
    Sambuca Molinari 248

DoC (Denominazione di Origine Controllata) 243, 246
DoCG (Denominazione di Origine Controllata e Garantita) 244, 246
Dolcetto (grape variety) 245
DoP Denominazione d'Origine Protetta (Protected Designation of Origin) 22
dough balls (Frittelle) 33
doughnuts (Bombolone) 214

eggs
    for Frittata Verde 156
    for Homemade Pasta 76
    Larder notes 25
Emilia-Romagna 122–3
Espresso Martini (cocktail) 240

Falanghina (grape variety) 244
Fave 179
Fegato alla Veneziana 129
Fernet Branca 248
Fiano (grape variety) 244
Finocchio (biscuit) 223
fish
    baccalà (salt cod), preservation of fish 34
    Branzino (Sea bass) 106
    Bruschetta con crema di baccalà mantecato 47
    Calamari Fritti 103
    Capesante (Scallops) 102
    Carpaccio di Pesce 37
    Larder notes 25
    Merluzzo (Cod) 105
    Pesce al Forno 114
    Pesce al Taglio 116
    Salsa di acciughe e pomodori 38
    Scampi (Langoustine) 101
    Sgombro (Mackerel) 109
    Spaghetti con Tonno 84
    Zuppe di Pesce 60
Florence 70–1
flour
    for Homemade Pasta 76
    Larder notes 25
Focaccia 209
Fontina cheese 40
Fragola Fra (cocktail) 232
Franciacorta, Lombardy 247
Frangelico 248
Frittata Verde 156
Fritti 35

Galletti (Mushrooms) 161
Gavi 247
Gewurztraminer (grape variety) 244
Giolittii, Rome 86
Gnocci Cacio e Pepe 88–9
Granchio (Crab) 115

Grappa Nonino 249
Gremolata 102
    Gremolata di Selina 128

Homemade Pasta 76-7

IGP Indicazione Geografica Protetta
    (Protected Geographical Indication) 22
IGT (Indicazione Geografica Tipica) 244
Integrity 21-2
Ischia 46, 111, 131

La Scala, Milan 201
Lago Maggiore 227
Lake Garda 200-01, 247
Lambrusco 247
L'Aperitivo Nonino 239
Larder notes 25-6
    butter 25
    eggs 25
    fish 25
    flour 25
    meat 25
    olive oil 26
    pepper 26
    salt 26
    tomatoes 26
Lazio 86-7
lemons
    Amalfi lemons 176
    Sorbetto al limone 188
lentils
    Salsiccia 135
    Zuppe di Lenticchie 65
Liguria 226-7
Limoncello Di Capri IGP 249
Limoncello spritz 239
Linguine ai Frutti di Mer 96
Lombardia 200-01
Lucca 70
Lugana (wine) 247

Macedonia 188
Malvasia (grape variety) 245
Mandorle (biscuit) 220
Mandorle Speziate 50
Marzipan 193
Matera, UNESCO site, Puglia 147
Maturano (grape variety) 245
meat
    Bollito Misto 136
    Brodo di Carne 68
    Carbonara 91
    Coniglio all'Ischitana 131
    Fegato alla Veneziana 129
    Stufato di Capra al Pecorino 143
    Larder notes 25

    Milanese 132
    Pollo 139
    Polpette 41
    Porchetta 140-2
    Ragù 125
    Salsiccia 135
    Stufato di Capri al Pecorino 143
    Sugo con carne 80
    Ossobuco 126
Melanzane alla Parmigiana 152
Melograno (Pomegranate) 176
Mercato di Mezzo, Bologna 122-3
Merluzzo (Cod) 105
Milanese 132
Minestra 57
Minestrone 59
Montepulciano (grape variety) 245
Mount Etna 170
Mount Vesuvius 110
Mozzarella di Bufala 182
Mozzarella in Carrozza 38
mushrooms
    Contadino (pasta) 92
    Galletti 161
mussels
    Cozze 113
    Linguine ai Frutti di Mare 96
    Zuppe di Pesce 60

Nebbiolo (grape variety) 246
Negroamaro (grape variety) 246
Negroni 235
Negroni Sbagliato 235
Nero d'Avola (grape variety) 246
Noci con Miele 50
Notte Nocino (cocktail) 233

Olio al rosmarino 73
olive oil
    foundation of cooking 21-2
    Larder notes 26
oranges
    Arancia 172
    Anguria 236
    Crema di arancia 199
    Sciroppo di arancia e zafferano 191
Orvieto 247
Ossobuco 126-8
Osteria del Tempo Perso, Ostuni 147
Osterio Francescana, Moderna 123
Ostuni, Puglia 146

Padua 48
Pandolce 213
Pane di Altamura DoP 147
Panettone 16
    in Pudding con Crema di arancia 199

Panna Cotta 196
Panzanella 185
Parco Nationale d'Abruzzo, Lazio e Molise 28
Pasta ai Peperoni 81
Pasta al Pomodoro 79
Pasta e Fagioli 58
Pastone 42–3
Pecorino (grape variety) 245
Peperoni 162
Pesce al Forno 114
Pesce al Taglio 116
Pesto alla Genovese 57
Picinisco, Frosinone 28–9
Piemonte 226–7
Pinot bianco (grape variety) 245
Pinot grigio (grape variety) 245
Pinot nero (grape variety) 246
Pisa 70
Pizza al Taglio 210–11
pizza dough 210–11
Pizzeria Brandi, Naples 110
polenta
    Polenta con Fontina 40
    Torta di Pistacchio 191
Polignano a Mare, Puglia 147
Pollo (Chicken) 139
Polpette (Meatballs) 41
Pomodoro fresco 79
Pompelmo (cocktail) 236
Porchetta (pork) 140–2
Portofino 227
potato
    Ceci e Patate (soup) 73
    Crema di Patate 129
Pozzuoli, Campania 110
Primitivo (grape variety) 246
Prosecco 247
Puglia 146–7
Puntarelle 180
Puttanesca (pasta) 95

Radicchio di Treviso 167
Ragù 125
risotto
    Arancini 53
    Ossobuco 126
    Risotto alla Milanese 128
Ristorante Piperno, Rome 86–7

Salsiccia 135
Sambuca Molinari 249
San Gimignano 70
Sangiovese (grape variety) 246
Sant' Eustachio, Rome 86
sauces
    Salsa di acciughe 180

Salsa di acciughe e pomodori 38
Salsa di menta 150
Salsa di noci 132
Salsa di peperoncini 35
Salsa di pomodoro 209
Salsa di salvia 140
Salsa Inglese 136
Salsa verde 105
Scampi (Prawns) 101
Sciroppo di arancia e zafferano 191
seafood
    Aragosta (Lobster) 119
    Cozze (Mussels) 113
    Granchio (Crab) 115
    Linguine ai Frutti di Mare 96
Sgombro (Mackerel) 109
Sicily 170–1
Siena 70, 71
Soave 247
Sofia's Olive Oil 26, 132, 209
Sorbetto al limone 188
Spaghetti con Tonno 84
spinach 158
    Melograno 176
    Polenta con Fontina 40
    Spinaci e Pomodori 106
Spritz 239
STG Specialità Tradizionale Garantite (Guaranteed Traditional Speciality) 22
Strudel 202
Stufato di Capra al Pecorino 143
Südtirol 200–1
sugo 41
    Butter 79
    con Carne 80

Taormina, Sicily 170–1
Tiramisù 195
tomatoes
    Bruschetta 45–6
    Butter sugo 79
    Crema di Pomodoro (soup) 63
    Larder notes 26
    Minestrone 59
    Panzanella 185
    Pasta di Pomodoro 79
    Pizza al Taglio 210
    Puttanesca 95
    Ragù 125
    Salsa di acciughe e pomodori 38
    Salsa di pomodoro 209
    San Marzano tomatoes with mozzarella 182
    Spinaci e pomodori 106
    Sugo 41
    Sugo con carne 80

Torta al Cioccolato 205
Torta di Fichi e Mandorla 189
Torta di Pistacchio 191
Torta di Ricotta 224
Trebbiano (grape variety) 245
Trentino–Alto Adige 200–1
Treviso 48
Tuscany 70–1

VdT (Vino da Tavola) 244
Veneto 48–9
Verdicchio (grape variety) 245
Verdure 151
Vermentino (grape variety) 245
Verona 48
Via Condotti, Rome 86
Viareggio 71
Vin Brulé 240
Vin Santo (Holy Wine) 247

walnuts
    Cavolfiore 181
    Noce con Miele 50
    Salsa di noce 132
watermelon (Anguria)
    Anguria (cocktail) 236
    Anguria e Caprino 169
    Granchio 115
wine 243–7
    classifications of 243–4
    grape varieties 244–6
    styles of 246–7

Zabaglione 204
Zeppole 216
Zucca (Pumpkin) 150
Zuccini (Courgette) 175
Zuppe di Lenticchie 65
Zuppe di Pesce 60